A JOHN CATT PUBLICATION

TAKING CONTROL

HOW TO PREPARE FOR OFSTED INSPECTION

PAUL GARVEY

First Published 2017

by John Catt Educational Ltd,
12 Deben Mill Business Centre,
Old Maltings Approach,
Melton, Woodbridge IP12 1BL

Tel: +44 (0) 1394 389850
Fax: +44 (0) 1394 386893
Email: enquiries@johncatt.com
Website: www.johncatt.com

ISBN: 978 1 911382 20 1

Set and designed by
John Catt Educational Limited

Contents

To my two wonderful daughters, Anne-Marie and Laura.

Taking Control
How to Prepare for Inspection

INTRODUCTION

I used to call you at 12.05, if you were a school I used to inspect.

If you have bought this book (and thank you!) you are likely to be in a school that will soon be on the opposite end of the phone from someone like me.

The knowledge that your next Ofsted inspector (OI), or HMI is likely to call very soon after 12.00 on the day before your inspection may be useful, but the knowledge about why they'll be calling at that time, what they must do themselves on that day, in preparation and what you should do that afternoon as a result, could be very useful indeed.

This book gives you the inside story on inspection. The Latin saying *'praemonitus, praemunitus'* loosely translates as 'forewarned is forearmed' and with inspections being enormously high stakes today, schools really do need to be forewarned and you really do need to be metaphorically armed to the proverbial teeth against your inspectors. Be under no illusion: inspection is a battle that can definitely be won and can definitely be lost.

> *Ofsted say you shouldn't do anything extra to your day-to-day activities to prepare for inspection and I – and every single one of the schools I've supported through their inspections and so many others – say that's mad!*

Ofsted won't allow their independent inspectors to offer advice to schools; thus Ofsted wouldn't allow me to both inspect and to write a book like this. I said 'used to call you', in my first sentence. Very recently, this reason caused me to have to stop inspecting, but it has allowed me to write *'Taking Control'*.

Ofsted have a large team of over 1500 OIs (Ofsted Inspectors, 70% of whom are serving professionals in schools) who could be licensed to offer exactly this advice but the organisation chooses instead to prevent this excellent workforce from doing so. Of course OIs do help and of those I know, both serving in schools and those who are independent OIs, all use their knowledge in some way to help schools, often unpaid. Ofsted's stance means this advice has to be given below the organisation's radar. That's not me. I'm just too open and honest about supporting schools to prepare for inspection. This book could not have been written by any of Ofsted's OIs who wish to continue to inspect, but it is a book that I hope many schools will find extremely useful.

Although Ofsted say you should not prepare for inspection, your inspectors will be making mental notes about the 'effectiveness of leadership and management' all through your inspection. They will be thinking 'has this leadership team got the capacity to effect further improvement in this school'. If it becomes clear that leaders at all levels don't know your school as well as your inspectors might like you to, it will cause you problems. The criteria for this are not laid down. Indeed the phrase; 'capacity for further improvement' is only actually mentioned once in the Ofsted handbook (Page 43, in the bullets for 'inadequate' for effectiveness of leadership and management). Nevertheless, it will overhang your inspection and if your inspectors feel that leaders are not well briefed and organised, this may well raise its head, if not for an 'inadequate' grade, then as a counterweight to 'Good'. It will supplement thinking around other reasons why effectiveness of leadership and management may not be judged as positively as you would like it to be judged. It is the first 'unknown unknown' for which you need to be prepared (see below).

It is leadership who need to be prepared. Classroom teachers and assistants have next to no need. This book will say that any extra inspection preparation pressure put on classroom teachers and their assistants by leaders – or by themselves, as teachers can be their own worst enemy sometimes – is unnecessary. The contribution of the school's teachers and teaching assistants, to their upcoming inspection has already been done, pre-inspection. **Nothing** teachers can do by teaching, brilliantly, or otherwise, during inspection will change your grade. That grade has already been determined by your results and the progress of your pupils, to date. Teachers and their assistants should therefore have their usual teaching days and do **nothing** extra to prepare for an inspection, beyond speaking positively with inspectors and following your school's policies.

I've emboldened the 'nothings', as they are so important for reducing Ofsted-teacher workload. Indeed, I'll argue later that the inclusion of 'teaching' in the grade for 'quality of teaching learning and assessment' is unnecessary and redundant. It adds worry for leaders and thus adds work for teachers.

However, I go further than believing that leaders in schools should prepare for inspection, I firmly believe that leaders can **take control** of the process.

'*Taking Control*' gives your school the best chance possible to get the inspection grade that you feel you deserve. It will enable you to construct powerful arguments that your OI/HMI will find difficult to counter. A feature of this book is a concentration on data, or 'information' as Ofsted now call data. Although Ofsted would like you to feel that leadership and management are the main focus of an inspection – and the weight of inspection should, rightly fall on their shoulders and not on the shoulders of teachers – data is king in an inspection.

RAISEonline (RAISE) will be replaced in July 2017 by ASP (Analyse School Performance). The tables, graphs and scatterplots will be familiar from RAISE for which you will have your own school access, as you have with RAISE. There will be increased functionality and more content e.g. you will have access to your data dashboard via ASP, which you haven't from RAISE, but the basic information remains the same. The analysis in 'Taking Control' which refers to RAISEonline content can be used with ASP content. Inspectors will still have access to previous RAISE reports as well. The terminology becomes awkward.

From now on. I'll refer to RAISEonline and its replacement, ASP as simply 'RAISE/ASP'.

If you know you are leading 'Good' school (Grade 2, or G2); you know your staff are doing a good job day-to-day and your parents and pupils say the same, but your RAISE/ASP data may be suggesting a possibility of otherwise; this book is for you.

If you are leading a 'Good' school, but you have made improvements from your last inspection and you want your inspectors to recognise that and feel that you may now be an outstanding school; this book is for you.

If you feel you are leading an outstanding school, ostensibly exempt from inspection, doing amazing things, but are worried by your recent RAISE/ASP, or that recent events, may preclude another Grade 1 (G1); this book is for you.

If you are leading a school that is Grade 3, or Grade 4 (G3, or G4) and you are improving from difficult times, but you need Ofsted to listen to what is now possible in the future; this book is also for you.

An important piece of knowledge for all schools is that the interpretation of every single criterion in the inspection handbook, is subjective. It is down to the interpretation of your inspectors. That's where this book can help.

My advice is to be forearmed and if your preparation is lacking, the Ofsted 'School Inspection Handbook' (the 'handbook') may well give your inspectors licence to find reasons to say you are not as good as you feel – and know – you are. The grade given to a school has to add up. Things have to satisfy a 'best fit' of subjective judgements around the criteria for those four grades. The quality assurance process at Ofsted does not give either OIs, or HMIs, the freedom to write that a school is 'Good' if the handbook criteria are not well enough satisfied and all HMI and lead OIs know this. But, it is possible for you to help them towards decisions by what you do before and during your inspection.

With the help of this book, you can cleverly help your lead OI/HMI to write the inspection report you would like to read. Inspectors are very well trained in the use of the handbook and to be blunt; you have to know that inspection handbook as well, if not better than your inspectors. Know it well enough to be able to quote from it to back your position.

I will refer to what is currently the most recent version of this handbook throughout 'Taking Control', but please check at www.gov.uk for the most up-to-date version. All references to the handbook are greyed and contain page and paragraph location. The current handbook can be found at:

> www.gov.uk/government/publications/school-inspection-handbook-from-september-2015

The handbook is an extremely detailed and rather arcane document, but schools must be familiar with its intricacies. If you are not, you will be faced with an HMI/OI that is and that can leave you vulnerable. I'll help you throughout with clear references to the parts that I think are most helpful to you.

TYPES OF INSPECTIONS
In state schools, inspections now come in two types. Section 5 and Section 8 inspections. Section 5 inspections last two days, and Section 8 inspections, one.

In 2005, these replaced earlier, 'Section 10' inspections from the section of the 'Schools Inspections Act 1996', in which they were established in law. More experienced (OK, older!) readers may remember those big teams descending upon your school, looking at every department, after you had spent the 6 week(!) lead-in time working yourselves silly to prepare.

Section 5 inspections in England are named after the section in the 2005 Education Act and are 2-day affairs, with (now) half a day's warning, or they will occur if a short, Section 8 inspection 'converts' to a full Section 5 inspection to investigate the possibility a grade other than the school continuing as 'good'.

In addition to Section 5 inspections, Section 8 of the same act of parliament gave the inspectorate the power to perform other, 1-day, inspections at any time and for any reason, at the discretion of Her Majesty's Chief Inspector of Schools (HMCI). These inspections are known as Section 8 inspections, or 'monitoring inspections'. In 2012, Section 8 'short inspections' of previously 'Good' mainstream schools were introduced. All good schools now receive short inspections, as do outstanding nursery, pupil referral units and special schools. Conversion could involve an extra day, or perhaps more.

Following a Section 5 inspection, schools are given a judgment of overall effectiveness: either Grade 1 (G1, outstanding), Grade 2 (G2, good), Grade 3 (G3, requires improvement) or Grade 4 (G4, inadequate). Schools receiving a Grade 4 and a proportion of those receiving a Grade 3 receive further Section 8 monitoring inspections until they are graded good – although conversion to academy status now complicates inspection timings. There are no grades given, following an unconverted Section 8, 'short', inspection, just a letter with the main inspection findings and saying that you remain a 'Good' school.

'Conversion' occurs when the lead inspector/inspection team, of a short section 8 inspection, thinks the school may no longer be a 'Good' school. The school, in the inspector's eyes, may seem better, or may seem to have declined in quality, from the last inspection. A full Section 5 team will then be called in to complete the inspection. The grade is not, however, at all certain to change and the school may remain as a 'Good' school, but it will get a fully graded Section 5 report if the in section 'converts'.

A lead inspector (LI), of both Section 5 inspections and Section 8 inspections, can be either a HMI (Her Majesty's Inspector of Schools, salaried to Ofsted), or an OI

(Ofsted inspector) who is independent of Ofsted and works on an ad hoc basis doing a number of inspections per year and these inspectors can be serving professionals in schools. 70% of OIs are now employed as senior leaders in schools.

It's a complex situation, generally very well known to senior leaders in schools, but a situation that is sometimes difficult for staff to know the full details. For the reasons why we have this split of Section 5 inspection/Section 8 'short' inspection of 'Good' schools, and the fact that G1 schools are exempt from regular inspection, see Chapter 1.3 Why Have We Not Been Inspected Yet?

'Taking Control' will aid those schools that need to persuade their OI/HMI that the short, Section 8, inspection of your currently 'Good' school really does need to convert to look at whether you are now an 'Outstanding' school.

Ofsted expect a Section 8, to come to a previously 'Good' school with the presumption that a school is still 'Good', but after reviewing your data, pre-inspection, all HMI/OIs will have formed initial ideas about your school that they will need to test out. However, they will not have made any judgements – promise! – long experience has taught me that you never know what you will find when you walk through the doors of a school. But always remember that all grades and criteria are subjective and your lead inspector has to evidence any decisions they make, to get their eventual Section 8 letter, or final Section 5 report, through quality assurance.

A very persuasive SEF (the acronym means 'Self-Evaluation Form' – though there is now no compulsory 'form' to fill in, as there was at the start of Section 5 inspections, in 2005. It is just a self-evaluation of your school, but 'SEF' survives in common parlance, so I'll use it as an abbreviation throughout) plus a confident demeanour from all leaders on inspection is needed. Combined with clear and accurate references to improvements, via your data and the inspection handbook, this can augment the positive thinking that a lead inspector may already have – that this could be a school that is now better than 'Good'. All they may need is the right help to convert that inspection. In addition, if they don't see you confidently helping them towards their decision, even though their pre-inspection view of your school is positive, your HMI/OI will be making unspoken value judgements about whether leadership and management are really driving improvement in an 'Outstanding' school, or whether they still have some way to go. **Take control**. Provide your lead inspector with all the information they need to make the decisions you want them to make and deliver all necessary information with confidence, belief and persuasiveness.

> 'Taking Control' will also help if you are a G2 school, undergoing a short, Section 8 inspection and you really don't want that inspection to convert (and effectively look at G3).

Ostensibly, short inspections don't convert to look at any grade. In reality, of course, they do and you will know which way your HMI/OI is leaning as they are tasked to keep you up to date with how the inspection is going. This is especially true at the end of the Section 8 day when you are told that the inspection will convert. The inspector will tell you why they are not convinced you are still a G2 school.

However, not all inspections that convert actually change grade. Indeed a significant number don't, even though conversion to a full Section 5 has occurred. In 2016, Ofsted stated that:

> 'Fifty three per cent of secondary schools retained their good grade at inspection this year compared to 50% of those inspected in 2014/15. For primary schools, 61% of good schools inspected this year retained their good grade compared to 64% last year.' But they also said; 'Forty seven per cent of short inspections converted to a full Section 5 inspection. Inspections of secondary schools were more likely to convert than primary schools. Of those that converted, 24% remained good and a further 18% improved to outstanding'.[1]

---

1. dera.ioe.ac.uk/26006/2/Maintained_schools_and_academies_inspection_outcomes_as_ at_31_December_2015.pdf

Of the 24%, that's either a big 'well done' to those schools that avoided G3, or it was a possible missed opportunity to convince and persuade, for those schools who were on the cusp of G1/G2. 'Taking Control' can help more schools to avoid G3 and more schools to gain G1.

Between the lead inspector converting the inspection and a full team coming in, those G2/G3 schools whose grade did not change gathered enough ammunition and information to persuade a full Section 5 team. That is a dreadfully stressful process. If those schools could have been more persuasive on the Section 8 day, they would not have had to endure a full Section 5.

There's a key aspect of inspection that demonstrates the insecurity of your HMI/OI. Your lead inspector will call in a team because they are not sure your school is good and they haven't collected enough information on the one-day inspection. In other words, those schools whose grade remained the same, but their lead inspector had in mind they may be a G3, missed a big trick in managing to persuade the individual leading inspector of that on their Section 8 day. 'Taking Control' will give you those tools of persuasion.

This is, perhaps, the most difficult inspection situation. The possibility of a grade slip from G2 to G3. This, as all presently 'Good' schools know, opens up the potential abyss of a forced conversion to an academy; perhaps being swallowed up and 'sponsored', by an academy chain which, if you had a choice, you would not consider joining. The choice of determining your own future in an academy-dominated educational world may be taken away from you; simply because of a cusp G3 decision, brought about through not knowing what you could have done to prepare fully. This can all too easily happen, if you can't show an inspection team that you were actually a 'Good ' school who had turned a data corner and the future is actually a lot brighter than your current RAISE/ASP data suggests. 'Taking Control' will give you the best chance possible of persuading your LI/HMI that you deserve another three years to encourage and to realise the potential of those green shoots. That would leave you as a G2 school, much more in control of your own future. High stakes indeed.

On the other side of the fence, so as to speak, academy chains and multi academy trusts (MATs) are under scrutiny from a government who expect results, in terms of school improvement. The main and very crude, measure that is being used to judge

MAT success are the changes in Ofsted grades of the schools that comprise the MAT or chain. As the MAT/chain will have been expected to assimilate a potential significant number of G3/G4 schools, it is then extremely important that the strongest possible arguments are offered to show the improvement of individual schools to inspection teams. An improving set of Ofsted grades over time, or a maintenance of existing 'Good' grades, is a very strong argument for Ofsted, in talks with the Regional Schools Commissioner, to not perform a full and potentially damaging, inspection of the MAT, or academy chain. **'Taking Control' is also for you**.

WHAT THIS BOOK CAN'T DO IS SAVE YOU

If your school does not give pupils a leg-up in their life chances, from joining your school to leaving, there's nothing this book can do to help you to change your likely Ofsted grade. If pupil progress from their starting points (a very important phrase – more later) is poor, by any measure – and this book will detail many ways that you use can show progress – something in your school has to change. You see, I do believe in a strong inspectorate that inspects for pupils. I support a professional inspection process and I agree with Ofsted on many things. If your pupils are not getting a good deal over time, please don't look to 'Taking Control', as your safe passage. If you are in that position, I would have had no hesitation in giving you a Grade 4 and I would expect your inspectors to do exactly the same.

However, if it is simply that you are finding it hard to demonstrate that the pupils in your school are getting a good deal over time, but actually staff, leaders, parents and pupils feel that they are; **this book is definitely for you**.

There is a moral base to the school inspection process, to which I and every other Ofsted inspector I have ever met, subscribe: I inspected for the pupils. Not for headteachers, not for senior leaders, not for teachers, or TAs, or for governors, or MAT boards. There was only one reason I inspected (the money is only reasonable, in recompense for the responsibility of leading, which is huge) and that was to ensure that the pupils in a school would get that best deal possible in the future. If myself and my teams, judged that pupils ought to be getting a better deal – following an extremely detailed and many-faceted inspection – we would walk away from the school knowing that we had done the best job we could have done for the pupils, even though the school would have been given a Grade 3, or a Grade 4.

Yes; things in that school may have to change. Yes; people may have to leave, as a result of the inspection – it may be leaders, initially, but perhaps later, teaching staff under a change of leadership. However, on inspection, you follow that moral imperative that the pupils come first. They only get one go at their education and an inspection that highlights problems in a school can help them to get the best out of the education they are offered. As I said in 'Talk for Teaching'[2], Headteachers and Principals are brilliant people, doing an extremely difficult and demanding job; indeed, I describe them all as 'mad', but some find that brilliance beyond them and that can impact upon pupils. In that case, it does not matter how much effort you put into inspection preparation, 'Taking Control' won't save you.

A Grade 4 is not in any way the worst thing that can happen to a school. It can give the school a baseline from which to change and move forward. Does anyone like working in a school that is clearly failing? No; however, if a school is not failing, but outside agencies such as the local authority, or the Regional School Commissioners office are applying pressure, by saying that it is failing, (and perhaps without an actual inspection) this book will help you with your arguments. Again, it will not save you if agendas are fixed, or your school really is poor, but there are organisations that may be able to help – especially the NAHT. (www.naht.org.uk)

Donald Rumsfeld's quote from 2002 rings so true here: He was talking about a very different circumstance and was actually using the 1955 work of two American psychologists, Joseph Luft and Harrington Ingham. His rather tortuous words, during a press interview for the U.S. Department of Defense news briefing on February 12, 2002, concerning the lack of evidence for 'weapons of mass destruction' in the Iraq war have become infamous:

> '...there are known knowns. These are things we know that we know. There are known unknowns. That is to say, there are things that we know we don't know. But there are also unknown unknowns. There are things we don't know we don't know.'

Therein lies the crux of what this book will help you to do. I've mentioned one

2. Garvey, P. (2017) Talk for Teaching. John Catt Educational Ltd., ISBN: 978 1 911382 09 6

possible 'unknown unknown' already, around capacity for further improvement and there will be many more. *'Taking Control'* will reveal those unknown unknowns, the lack of knowledge about which could potentially cost you dearly on inspection. You will never know the degree to which your lack of knowledge about such unknown unknowns will have damaged your defence, if they have. However, with those unknown unknowns revealed, it becomes possible for you to have the confidence to **take control** of your inspection and to present your arguments in the most cogent and persuasive way possible...

From now on, the book is divided into three main sections entitled:

Section 1: Pre-inspection.
Section 2: SEF Writing.
Section 3: An Inspector's Inspection – During and After Your Inspection.

In these three sections, you will uncover unknown unknowns bespoke to you. I can't point each one out, as your personal unknown unknowns are, logically, unknown unknowns to me! Some information will be known to you and some you might be hoping to find, but no-one except yourself will understand when you have discovered a little nugget of an 'unknown unknown'!

SECTION 1:
PRE-INSPECTION

1.1 Pre-inspection: Be a Great School

First and foremost: be a great school. Here, I agree with Ofsted completely. If your school is a great school, you have no need to worry about Ofsted and absolutely no need to do anything extra to prepare. Please pass this book on to a school who may need it. Such schools as yours just need to carry on doing what they are doing and continuing to improve. I know a few schools who do not complete a self-evaluation as such. They have no need. Instead, they have the confidence, data and conviction that any inspection team won't miss that they do things in an excellent way. What those schools do is nothing short of remarkable, year, after year, after year. There is no set pattern, or format, that makes them remarkable; just a vision of excellence that brings everyone on board with leadership to achieve a common purpose – excellent progress for pupils. That vision and common purpose leads to large and small comprehensives, with, or without sixth forms being excellent, nursery, infant, junior and primary schools being excellent, very traditional schools being excellent, Montessori schools being excellent, Grammars and Steiner schools being excellent... I could go on. There is #nobestwayoverall here (Twitter hashtag!), all can be successful with great vision and purpose (as I also believe there is #nobestwayoverall in how to teach). There is just excellent leadership and a vision that fits the context of the school to a 'T'. If that is you, please put this book down and do something else more worthwhile. You don't need 'Taking Control' or my help: you are already firmly in control.

Most of these schools are already 'Outstanding' schools and may have maintained excellence for many years. They are also exempt from inspection. I believe this is now an anachronism that Ofsted need to address. Some of these schools have not been inspected for over a decade. Some of them have certainly continued to be excellent of course, however, some of those G1 schools may have problems developing that are not easily, or yet, revealed in RAISE/ASP data, or known to parents. Who would know this before a crisis came, now there is no inspection of G1 schools?

It is my personal belief that all schools should now be inspected and also that the 'Outstanding' grade should be removed from the Ofsted handbook. In my view, schools should be judged to be either providing a good education, or not. Parents' perceptions of what is an outstanding school for their children are often very different to the 'Outstanding' criteria, as set out in the Ofsted handbook anyway. If a school is judged to be providing a good standard of education, let's then allow parents to chose their school, based upon information the school provides. They will have the security of Ofsted's stamp of 'Good' approval, without the worry, or perception that, if a school is 'Good', it could still be somehow quite a way from being 'good enough' – but actually, that school may turn out to be perfect, for their child.

Schools also know that an outstanding badge will exempt them from inspection, as long as their pupil outcomes remain pretty good and they have no major safeguarding concerns that Ofsted judge to be 'qualifying concerns'. Such concerns are down to Ofsted to decide. There are no published criteria – yet – for them. A 'qualifying concern' would cause senior HMI to send in an inspection team.

Notwithstanding, my own objections to the grade of 'Outstanding', I'm a realist. G1 is not going to disappear overnight and the badge currently confers significant weight in MAT discussions. Hence this is a very good reason to be very inspection-persuasive if you are a G2/G1 cusp school! *'Taking Control'* **will help schools in your position.**

1.2 Pre-inspection: Progress Since Your Last Inspection

Immediately following your inspection, ensure you address what your inspection team asked of you. No matter what grade you are, those; 'What does the school need to do to improve further?' points may come back to haunt you if you are not seen to have acted upon then and indeed, if you cannot show that you have improved. Even if you are a G2 school and were inspected over five years ago, it would not be sensible to think that you can safely ignore these. You can't.

I have to mention that you may find that there is some silliness in some 'points for improvement' from around 5-6 years ago, deriving from inspectors being asked to be time specific around improvement points with short time limits. We were asked to ask schools to make improvements in around 12-18 months. It was supposed to provide an exhortation from Ofsted that improvements should be rapid. Unfortunately, it led to the farcical situation where inspectors were writing 18-month timescales for improvement for 'Good' schools that were not going to be inspected for at least three years and sometimes five! Who would monitor the improvement (or not) at the end of the written timescale? I've just been looking at one of my old reports for a primary school where I'd asked them, to improve something by summer 2012. I'm smiling, as they were not inspected again until 2016! You can safely ignore those, frankly, daft time limits, but you can't ignore the improvement points.

I will detail the ways in which improvement could be demonstrated later in the book, but these points for improvement from your previous inspection need to be explained fully under a sub-heading in your self-evaluation. If your SEF explanation is cogent and you can show that improvement is clear, it is highly unlikely that your HMI/OI will not make them an area for detailed exploration. You may not even be asked about them. There will be other inspection trail fish for your inspector(s) to fry! However, if you skip over these, then you find that you are suddenly having to scramble around for evidence to show that improvement has happened, you are laying yourself open to an issue developing that could cost you.

This is where your previous lead inspector can have been at his, or her best. If you are a G3/G4 school, your points for improvement, maybe with some discussion, will be set by your team. They are often plentiful and often too many. Their number was determined by the writing expectations and quality assurance process. Your lead inspector will have known that any criticism of the school had to be followed up in a point for improvement and as G3 and G4 schools often have a range of poorer areas, there may be a plethora of points for improvement.

However, if you were a G2 school, you may well have been able to work with your lead inspector to formulate areas for improvement that were most useful to you. This was an excellent approach used by many leads. I did and I confess I often exchanged next-day emails with HTs of schools I'd just inspected as 'Good' or 'Outstanding', to ensure the correct wording on areas for improvement. I truly found them so hard to formulate at the end of a second day, when I was usually shattered and my brain was turning to mush! If your HMI/LI worked with you, improvements in those areas really should be easy to evidence, as they will have been areas in which you knew you needed to improve.

If you are a G4 school, you will have produced an action plan around these improvement points, which will have been monitored by HMI. This is often a very useful and supportive process, led by some excellent HMI who really care about the improvements you are making. Ofsted usually provide time for these HMI to revisit and revisit, until they feel that the school has improved sufficiently and is ready for a full inspection. Recently, forced inspection has got in the way of this process and if the school is an 'orphan' school, that no sponsor seems to want to take on, school improvement can be badly delayed, especially if the headteacher leaves and an interim head is appointed. Even after assimilation by a new and perhaps unwanted, multi academy trust, school improvement can prove very difficult as the school has effectively been cast out of the Ofsted support net.

If you are a G3 school, the picture is less clear. You may have been asked to produce an action plan by your Local Authority and you may have received support and monitoring from an HMI. If you have, you were lucky and in all the RI cases I've known, support has been spoken of highly and has had excellent effect. The point of that HMI help is to support schools to get to 'Good'. However, almost three years on, some of these schools have received no monitoring visit and others only one early on in their RI life. This is an area where a lack of HMIs could have been supported by Ofsted's OIs and it has been an opportunity missed. If these schools are then re-inspected, have received no support and are given RI again, what responsibility should Ofsted take for the grade remaining the same?

Those schools needed support and I've been privileged to support some who have subsequently gained G2 at their next inspection. However, for Ofsted not to offer regular monitoring support to these schools and then say they should not seek support from people trained in inspection procedures, is in my view, unfair.

In their support role, HMI provide, often excellent, school support with the expressed outcome that the school should be good at its next inspection. There aren't however, enough HMI to do this for all G3 schools, whereas Ofsted have a team of 1200, well trained, non-HMI who could do that very well outside of Ofsted, but forbids them to do so. In actuality, they do and the Ofsted-trained senior leaders offer support in their own schools, across their multi academy trusts and in school-to-school support. I know they do, because I work with them. Other independent OIs do offer support, but it has to be offered under the Ofsted radar, or else! I was found out – fair enough; it was a 'fair cop guv', but there are always silver linings and parting company with Ofsted allowed me to write this book!

If you are a G4 school, you must arrange your inspection preparation mainly around your areas for further improvement that were identified by your inspection team and such preparation has to start immediately following inspection. Concentrate also on demonstrating that pupils' are safe and that through your data, their progress is accelerating. If you are a G3 school, you must have your improvement points as a major pillar of your preparation depending upon how you are monitored. In addition, also concentrate on demonstrating that pupils are safe and that, through your data, pupils' progress is accelerating. If you are a G2 school, ensure you have sufficient evidence to show improvement since your last inspection, but there's no need for these improvement points to dominate your preparation. Instead, concentrate mainly on demonstrating that your current pupils are safe and that they are making progress.

You'll see a clear theme in that last paragraph, which must occupy a very important part of your preparation for your next inspection. **Next to safeguarding, progress is king**.

1.3 Pre-inspection: Why Have We Not Been Inspected Yet? (It's Down To Money, Of Course!)

There are arguments that schools shouldn't be inspected, that they should simply be subject to just an annual data risk assessment by Ofsted and given a grade that is reviewed every year. I don't subscribe to those views, indeed, I'd rather see all schools, including those given the badge of 'Outstanding', inspected on a regular cycle, notwithstanding their data, or their grade. However, cost savings over the last six years have forced Ofsted along this route of longer time periods between inspections and proportionate inspection, depending upon the school's grade. Ofsted call this effective transfer of inspection responsibilities to an HMI's desk 'risk assessment' and they apply it to all schools. It is far cheaper than inspection.

If you are an 'Outstanding' school, or a 'Good' school, then waiting for your next inspection can get wearing – even if you are 'exempt'. I know Ofsted's view is that schools shouldn't prepare for inspection, but the schools I support feel strongly that this view is not sensible. I believe it is naïve.

G2 schools, notwithstanding risk assessment, are being moved to an Ofsted regime where they are inspected every three years. However, an inspection after 3 years is not usual. It is taking longer than that. In February 2016, writing in Ofsted's blog, Sean Harford, National Director of Ofsted wrote:

> '...with this academic year being a transitional one, it means that we will not be in the 'three-year cycle' for all 'Good' schools straight away – we will be moving towards it.[3]

On Twitter, on 22/02/2017, Sean said; 'At current inspection rate 'approx 3 yrs' will be by 18/19.[4] The timeframe is being regularly extended.

Statute dictates that a G2 school must be inspected before the end of the fifth academic year after the previous inspection. Thus there are 'Good' schools that have not been inspected for over five years and they are wondering where Ofsted are. Ofsted's National director also said, introducing the above blog comment, over a year ago;

---

3. educationinspection.blog.gov.uk/2016/02/08/inspection-timescales/

4. twitter.com/HarfordSean/status/834405907530387456

'There's been some speculation about the timing of inspections, particularly of the new short inspections, and I understand that some schools may be anxious about where they are.'

I can assure him that they still are anxious!

The reasons for the backward pedalling on the date for the achievement of this target of inspecting all G2 schools within three years are obvious. It is a lack of inspectors, especially HMI and a lack of money. I predict it will be quite a while until Ofsted achieve that inspection time-target of 'approximately three years' and as such, G2 schools may well need to continue to maintain 'inspection ready' for a long time, often through changes of key personnel. That's difficult – unless, of course, specific preparation for your inspection is, as Ofsted would like to believe it should be, unnecessary.

G1 schools are exempt from inspection, but evidence from the Education Policy Institute (below) shows this has not to be the case for a significant proportion of these schools. Their research indicates that the average inspection wait time for an 'Outstanding' school it is actually four years. If you are an 'Outstanding' school that now has waited almost ten years to be inspected – and you have no idea when you will be inspected again – you'll find that the inspection playing field you will have to negotiate has changed considerably. New senior staff and maybe a new headteacher (or a succession of several) may bring with them recent inspection experience, but in ten years a school can change enormously in vision and context. Isn't this in itself a reason to inspect outstanding schools regularly? Again, money dictates and it will be interesting to see whether Ofsted ever move away, or have the resources to move away, from their position that 'Outstanding' schools should be exempt from inspection.

Exempt; though it may sound an enviable place to be (if you are a school that isn't exempt), it may not be not the easiest of positions to occupy. There are 'Outstanding' schools who wish to be inspected regularly. The noose of expectation can tighten with time.

To save money, a regime of 'proportionate inspection' was introduced in 2012. The government rationale was that regular inspection was considered an unnecessary burden on our highest-performing schools. However, Estelle Morris, the then shadow Education Secretary, recognised that cost saving was the driving force behind proportionate inspection. In 2011 she said in a Guardian article that; *'Only the treasury benefits from the proposal to waive future inspections for schools that Ofsted judges outstanding'.*[5]

In 2012, Ofsted's budget was reduced by over 10% from £200m to £176m (see the figures on P8 of their 2014 strategic plan[6]). Estelle Morris' 2011 comment, in my opinion, remains true. Since the time of that comment, all Ofsted's tinkering with inspection timings have almost certainly been driven by a cost-saving imperative. In the 2015-16 tax year, treasury figures show that Ofsted's budget was eventually again reduced by £27.8m to £134.6m, from £162.4m the previous year.[7] That's a reduction of 1/3 in Ofsted's budget in the four years since 2012. A swingeing cut in anyone's book. Ofsted is very unlikely to escape further cuts so watch this space for possible further reductions in costly, face-to-face, inspections.

In November 2016, The Education Policy Institute (EPI) produced a fascinating and well-researched report written by Jo Hutchinson and entitled *'School inspection in England: Is there room to improve?'*. In it, she details the average times from previous inspection to most recent for all (Ofsted) grades of school. She says:

> *'Before considering how many years have elapsed since the latest Ofsted inspection for schools that have since deteriorated, we begin by looking at the average time since their latest inspection for all schools. Due to Ofsted's risk management approach and prioritisation of weaker schools, those with better judgements typically have longer periods between inspections. The time elapsed since the latest inspection is very similar for primary and secondary schools.*
>
> *For schools judged 'Outstanding' at their last full inspection, the time elapsed since that inspection ranges from less than a year to around eight years, with an average of four years. Up to four years (NB; actually up to six years) have passed since the last inspection for schools judged 'Good', with an average of two years.*

---

5. www.theguardian.com/education/2011/nov/21/ofsted-inspections-outstanding-schools-exempt

6. www.gov.uk/government/uploads/system/uploads/attachment_data/file/379920/Ofsted_2 0Strategic_20Plan_202014-16.pdf

7. www.parliament.uk/documents/commons-committees/Education/Estimates-Memoranda/ Ofsted-2015-16-Main-Estimates-Memorandum.pdf

Schools judged 'Requires improvement' at their last inspection have not received a Section 5 inspection for up to two years, with an average of just over a year. Up to three years have passed since the last Section 5 inspection of schools judged 'inadequate', with an average of a year.

The pattern of longer waiting times since the latest inspection for some schools judged 'inadequate' than those judged 'Requires improvement' is explained by 'inspection holidays' for schools that have become sponsored as a response to poor performance, to give them time to deliver improvements.[8]

This current system has left some 'Good' schools without an inspection for nearly six years. If they convert to being an academy towards the end of that inspection time, they will now be inspected 'as soon as possible', according to Sean Harford.[9]

If possible, this inspection will take place still within the statutory timeframe for unconverted schools. In addition to this, we have the continuing situation where a G1 school may never be inspected again. Is this healthy?

In a speech to the Association of School and College Leaders (ASCL) conference in 2014, the idea of 'light touch' inspections of 'Good' schools was proposed by Sir Michael Wilshaw, with all G2 schools having a short visit by an inspector 'every 2-3 years'.[10] It morphed into the short inspection regime, but the '2-3 years' part has not proved achievable. Cost again.

Estelle Morris asked a pertinent question in her Guardian article:

'If, however, I am wrong and ministers really are going to give up all their centralised powers, let's just see what happens the first time a previously high-performing school hits the headlines – and hasn't been inspected for a decade.'[11]

Estelle; you were right and it is already happening!

---

8.   epi.org.uk/wp-content/uploads/2016/11/school-inspection-in-england-web.pdf
9.   twitter.com/HarfordSean/status/861667375254560769
10. www.gov.uk/government/news/new-way-of-inspecting-good-and-outstanding-schools-proposed
11. www.theguardian.com/education/2011/nov/21/ofsted-inspections-outstanding-schools-exempt

This annual risk assessment already happens for all schools, but currently it is a two-stage process. The first stage involves a desktop 'risk assessment' of a school, which involves looking at RAISE/ASP data, 'Inspection Dashboard' data and KS5 data. If concerns about publicly available data are found, a more in-depth, review by HMI takes place at Ofsted. There are currently no benchmarks for this. Ofsted has obfuscated here for a long time (too long) and hasn't released their data triggers for the second stage of the process. This appears to be about to change. On March 17th 2017, Sean Harford said, on Twitter,[12] 'We are soon to publish the basis for our risk assessment'. That will be welcomed and it is not before time. I asked the question of 'how long?', to which he replied 'weeks', so by the time this book is published, you may have the answer.

As a result of this obfuscation, schools have been left worried and anxious that a one-year, easily explained, dip in their headline data could lead to an inspection with only half a day's notice in which they run the risk of dropping a grade. This could be catastrophic for the school, in the current high stakes academy climate. Not to prepare fully, if your previous year's RAISE/ASP data looks poorer than the previous year's data, could be a very risky path to take.

Ofsted examine your data every year, but do not have access to all the data you would present on inspection, only your data that is publicly available. They make decisions based upon on that data as to whether they should consider you for inspection and then inspect, but don't tell you their rationale. Then they tell you not to prepare for your inspection, during which they will ask you detailed questions about your data to which they expect you to answer convincingly on the spot.

Would you expect your pupils not to prepare for their SATs, GCSEs, or A-levels? Not in a million years. Instead, you support those pupils in preparing for their tests. I believe that saying to schools not to prepare for their inspection is an untenable position for Ofsted to take. I do support Ofsted in most areas, but this is one where I can't agree. Not all schools need to prepare, but most do. If your school is one, I hope this book helps you greatly in doing so.

---

12. twitter.com/HarfordSean/status/861468437973000192

1.4 Pre-inspection: School reviews; the Importance of Having an External Eye

As part of your preparation, I feel is very important that you get an external eye on your school. This is best done as part of your annual self-evaluation cycle, so all leaders and staff are used to the process. It should mirror inspection. Whoever you employ to do this should have recent – or current, if you can manage it without Ofsted spotting them – experience of leading inspections. To use peer review is only good up to a point and I'm no fan, unless the peer team is buttressed by inspection steel. When it comes to the crunch of giving you truly pertinent advice, perhaps with difficult messages upon which you'll need to act, does a fellow and perhaps neighbouring, headteacher have the strength to give you that tough advice that you may need?

With luck and if you are not already an academy, your local authority (LA) will have such people who can review you well and a review may be part of an annual cycle. However, LAs have agendas around inspection and can be very defensive in writing review reports and judging grades, ensuring their own backs are covered. Some strong and successful LAs can stand up to outside influence better than others and I know some excellent people who still work for local authorities. Other good quality LAs work well and in tandem with their Regional Schools Commissioner and that relationship is set to develop further.

However, some schools tell horror stories about weak local authorities. No wonder they are weak, as budget cuts have forced smaller local authorities to shrink their school services so almost no one is left. Without enough personnel, such local authorities now commission much of their school monitoring and improvement work from teaching schools, or outside agencies. Tales of a lack of LA support, unfair LA grades and draining LA improvement plans abound. multi academy trusts (MATs) have taken over this monitoring role from LAs, but if you are a MAT CEO reading this, please don't assume that the strengths in leadership in your MAT equip the MAT to peer-review your schools sufficiently well, unless they inspect and lead Ofsted inspections. An outside eye, with recent Ofsted experience (or current, if they can work under Ofsted's radar), is very useful.

NO 'MOCKSTEDS'

Please don't put teachers under pressure; there is no need. There should not be a 'Mocksted', which would involve reviewing the quality of teaching and learning. There's very little a review team could add to your knowledge of who is teaching well and who isn't, over the course of a couple of days. The term 'Mocksted' is rightly reviled from past poor practice, because of the extra pressure it has put on teachers. However, I'll argue in 'Taking Control' (chapter 2.5 SEF Writing: Quality of Teaching, Learning and Assessment) that teachers can do little to affect the outcome of an inspection during the inspection itself; their inspection contribution is already done and written in the school's results to date. So why pay good money for someone to review your teachers, unless it really is to give bespoke, individual support, to those that aren't performing well?

Save your money there and target support where it could be useful. Provide professional development for all and the best (and the cheapest) professional development is to put it in the hands of your teachers and get them into each other's classrooms. 'Talk for Teaching'[13] will help you to do this. Don't use outside help to assess your teachers. Trust yourselves; you know best here. Assess your own teachers within your school. You work most closely with them on a daily basis. SLT/HT/Principal knows their strengths and weaknesses as teachers best. Coach those who aren't doing well and provide professional development and individualised coaching to help them to improve. No 'Mocksteds', please! Concentrate, instead, on an annual review, targeted at school leaders, to both test the temperature of your school and to coach and prepare those leaders in how best to face inspection.

13. Garvey, P. (2017) Talk for Teaching. John Catt Educational Ltd., ISBN: 978 1 911382 09 6

1.5 Pre-inspection: Data is King

Don't you just love trying to find the correct grammatical use of 'data' in an idiom, or otherwise! I go with The Guardian's style guide here. 'Data takes a singular verb (like agenda), though strictly a plural; no one ever uses "agendum" or "datum"'. Ofsted agree with this use in their house style.[14]

If, for you, data takes a plural verb; 'data are king' is not wrong, but for me;

'Data is King!'

Actually, progress is king and if your HMI, or lead OI, go down the path of talking too much about your attainment data, remind them of the Ofsted handbook and the grade criteria contained therein. These clearly state, again and again, that it is **progress** they should be looking at and not attainment. Within progress, inspectors must do the following when judging 'outcomes for pupils' (Page 53, Paragraph 175):

> *'In judging achievement (i.e. outcomes for pupils), inspectors will give most weight to pupils' progress. They will take account of pupils' starting points in terms of their prior attainment and age when evaluating progress. Within this, they will give most weight to the progress of pupils currently in the school, taking account of how this compares with the progress of recent cohorts, where there are any. Inspectors will consider the progress of pupils in all year groups, not just those who have taken or are about to take examinations or national tests. As part of pupils' progress, inspectors will consider the growth in pupils' security, breadth and depth of knowledge, understanding and skills.'*

---

14. www.gov.uk/government/uploads/system/uploads/attachment_data/file/596603/
GuideToOfstedHouseStyle.pdf

The focus on progress applies to progress across early years, progress from entry to the phonics screening check and progress across KS1 – crucially important for Infant schools. It will also apply in the future to the newly announced 'Times Tables check', that pupils will sit for the first time in 2019. (Fortunately, it won't now apply to SATs at 7: hurrah! Who really thought that was a good idea?) None of these have published, aggregated progress measures (yet) with which to compare to national (there is the fairly crude measure at KS1 of the number of pupils who gain/don't gain 'expected', or 'greater depth' from EYFS profile measures outcomes). Instead, they all have attainment measures and your HMI/OI has to acknowledge these pupils' starting points in all those areas and the progress your pupils have made from their various starting points. If they won't do that; complain immediately. Progress is also completely pertinent from pupils' entry points, to leaving, in middle schools. Inspection in a 9-13 school must never focus solely on the only publicly available data that is, of course, from KS2 at 11 only.

In primary schools, progress must not be inspected just across KS2, though that is the only national, fully aggregated progress data for primary and junior schools on RAISE/ASP. Nor must progress be inspected only from KS2 to GCSE in secondary schools, though there is no published KS3 progress measure. Schools can also evidence progress within each of their year groups. This can be an important weapon in your armoury to show that your previous year's RAISE/ASP was actually a blip and in other year groups, pupils may be bounding ahead. Remember that the main Ofsted inspection measure is progress from pupils' **starting points** to their attainment upon leaving the school. In primary schools, especially, progress **must not** only be judged across KS2 and if your HMI, or OI, is trying to do that, again; complain immediately.

The order of inspection areas in the Ofsted handbook might lead you to believe that second to the judgement for 'overall effectiveness', the judgement of 'effectiveness of leadership and management' is key. Ofsted and the previous HMCI, Michael Wilshaw, have been publicly very clear that is the case. Believe that at your peril. The 'quality (and hopefully, therefore, the effectiveness) of leadership and management' can certainly be a factor in boosting, or anchoring, your grade, as can other inspection areas, especially safeguarding, but your inspectors will look first at the 'outcomes for pupils' data they receive. On inspection, data is king and safeguarding is queen! This won't be a surprise to, probably, all schools and probably not you as a reader. Ofsted haven't been successful in convincing schools of the paramountcy of leadership and management in inspectors' thinking and that's simply because it is not paramount!

DATA RECEIVED BY A LEAD INSPECTOR PRIOR TO INSPECTION

Before visiting your school, the person leading your inspection will receive several things from Ofsted and will be expected to look at some others. It's important you are aware, as you can use this information in your preparation. A full list of all the information they receive is on Page 11, Paragraph 29 of the inspection handbook.

In terms of data, your lead inspector will receive your previous two RAISE reports or access to ASP after summer 2017. If you have a sixth form, they will receive your level 3 value added report. Nothing else. No FFT data, no ALPS data and no data from other commercial packages. That can give you an edge, as inspectors are tasked to look at **all** data/information produced by the school and your other data may contradict, or show a different picture to, the progress data in RAISE/ASP. The handbook is very clear on this point (Page 23, Paragraphs 77 and 79):

> 'During inspection, inspectors should consider performance information presented by the school for current pupils across year groups and previous cohorts, including that provided by external organisations. They should also consider the published data available to them before the inspection.'

And:

> 'Inspectors should consider a wide range of information. No **single measure** or indicator should determine judgments' (my emboldening).

There is nothing in the handbook that says that inspectors must use RAISE/ASP data in preference to, or in priority to, other data. There is a widespread and persistent myth that RAISE/ASP data takes priority, but that is simply not the case.

Your own data may be more discriminatory than RAISE/ASP in showing the progress of different groups, or in showing the improvements in rates of progress over time. It may prioritise different aspects of your data in summaries, or conclusions, from the bald summary presented on your data dashboard. Your data dashboard may have more negative statements than, perhaps, your data is deserves, due to the algorithm for its production picking up sig- information for very small groups. Or it can give you a double, or triple whammy, by incorporating a single piece of negative data in several entries.

An example of this would be if you have a few, low ability SEND pupils who, for particular reasons, cognitive, or medical, haven't progressed well and didn't attend well. As a result, the effects of these few pupils can show, on your Inspection Dashboard, several times. In a secondary, this also can affect your EBacc element, as well as your overall. The irony is that you can't see the data for these few pupils, or know exactly how many they are, as RAISE/ASP does not discriminate far enough to pick up 'low ability SEND'. Thus the effects of these pupils may show several times as negative statements on your Inspection Dashboard, without you being able to see the data for these pupils! The only way to see how many you have and how they performed is to use the interactive version of RAISE/ASP and look at the individuals themselves.

Use your own, different data to RAISE/ASP, as often as you wish and if your HMI/ OI will not recognise their provenance, or conclusions and wants to focus only upon RAISE/ASP data; complain immediately.

Your lead inspector and the team, will also be expected to look at your website, so contextualise and explain any raw data you have there. Write these website explanations to match your SEF, not your school development plan, which may contain more reference to weaknesses.

They will also be expected to do an Internet check to look for any other publicly available information about the school that has made the news and any other publicly available information from other parties, such as the Regional Schools Commissioner (RSC), local authority (LA), the Department for Education (DfE), or the police. In addition, they will receive your previous inspection report/monitoring letters, responses from 'Parent View' and information about any qualifying complaints to Ofsted, which may include information about safeguarding issues and warning notices issued to schools. That's a lot of work, so if you can include a paragraph in your SEF that says; 'there is no negative information, safeguarding, or otherwise, of which we are aware, on the Internet, or in the local press, from the RSC, LA, DfE, or police, concerning our pupils', it may help your lead inspector in verifying to them that their search is accurate. I always worried that I'd missed something and how many pages of Google should you check, as a lead inspector?

Beyond the data referred to above, your inspectors will have nothing more. That makes your self-evaluation so important, because this will be the first proper flavour of your school that your lead inspector (by far the most important person on the team and the individual who should be the main focus of your persuasion) will see. They need to see that before they visit and as early as possible on the afternoon following their introductory phone call to you.

Some schools have a separate 'Ofsted portal', via which inspectors are given access to documents. Be careful here; if this contains information that shouldn't be seen pre-inspection, it could compromise some of your hard work in building your argument via your SEF. I think a password-protected 'Ofsted portal can be a good idea, but vet the contents of the documentation that is uploaded to this area carefully, before giving your inspectors access. It is the SEF that your lead inspector needs to see first.

1.6 Pre-inspection: Self-Evaluation and its Importance in the Presentation of 'King' Data

This heralds one of the most important pre-inspection tasks: the writing of a self-evaluation. It is quite possible to go into an inspection without a self-evaluation, if you are supremely confident about your inspection outcome, but few schools do. In my view, schools are very sensible to write a self-evaluation to inform their inspectors (a SEF), and to send it over to the inspector as soon as possible after the initial phone call. It is especially important in the presentation of your pupil outcomes, i.e. your data, or as Ofsted now term this: your 'performance information'. There's a whole section on self-evaluation coming up and there are dialogic tools to help both primary and secondary schools to write self-evaluations in appendices 1 and 2 respectively. These should be used in tandem with that section.

Your self-evaluation is the first chance you have to set your **data, or performance information**, in the context of your school and your pupils. If you write your SEF in convincing, cogent and proud language, it can already have made a big difference to your lead inspector's thinking when they drive through the gates of your school. I have already said that *'Taking Control'* can't save you, if our data shows you really aren't doing a good enough job, but the information in here, concerning self-evaluation, will go a long way towards helping you to present the most persuasive argument you can around data and I've already said that 'data is king'. This is especially true if you are a 'cusp' school (i.e. you could easily be one grade, or another, by the Ofsted handbook criteria) and always remember: all judgements are subjective.

Your SEF should root **your** thinking about your data into your lead inspector's thinking before they arrive. Indeed, for me, that is the single purpose of a SEF.

SECTION 2:
SEF WRITING

2.1 SEF Writing:
Writing a Persuasive Self-Evaluation, or SEF

> *A SEF, for me has only one final purpose.*
> *To put an idea into the mind of your lead inspector that*
> *you deserve the grade that you feel you are worth.*

Evaluate your school regularly. Update your SEF regularly as a result. Use your SEF as a working document with stakeholders to see the positives about where you are and where you are going. All fine. But don't forget that your SEF will have a singular audience on the afternoon prior to your inspection. For me, you are writing your SEF, primarily, to persuade your lead inspector. I believe that any other use of your SEF is secondary to that.

It is a view that will come as a surprise, or even a shock, to some and a view that Ofsted probably won't like, but it is a view developed from working with well over a hundred schools on self-evaluation and Ofsted preparation. It is also a view developed from inspecting many schools. Your SEF is crucial to your preparation and also to your lead inspector's preparation. It can put you at a disadvantage if it is written naively, or badly. Inspectors are human and they will make mental judgements when reading your SEF.

Please get someone to proof read your SEF! I've read some shockers when inspecting, which are littered with spelling and grammatical errors. It's not that leaders' grammar is poor; it's a lack of proof reading. Everyone makes mistakes, but this sets a bad example for the school leadership whose job it is to encourage good English and grammar via drafting, checking and re-drafting, amongst pupils. Be humble and get someone to proof read your SEF for you. I've also read shockers in a different way, that told me about every weakness that the schools had in great detail. Both 'shockers' could have had influence and when I saw examples of the second, I've just smiled when I've read them, thought; 'thank you very much' and wrote my inspection trails from them. Neither of the 'shockers' affected my eventual judgements, but you don't know your lead inspector's possible prejudices. Although inspector quality increased, following the 2015 cull and the change to inspectors being contracted directly to Ofsted, why even risk such a thing? Write your SEF intelligently and cleverly, to persuade and then get a 'gate-keeper' to check it. The English department, or a Y6 teacher is usually a safe bet!

A SEF must be honest, but to a point: your SEF should not present your lead inspector with their inspection trails on a platter. Let them work for those! Use and update your self-evaluation regularly. Every good school evaluates their progress. It is a necessary element of school improvement, but through those evaluations, have the overall SEF purpose firmly in mind. Set up a template that can be very quickly updated, in no more than an hour, following your initial phone call.

In my view your self-evaluation should sit alongside your school development plan (SDP), but definitely should **not** be combined with it. Your SDP will have your main areas of focus within its pages and these will give your inspection trails to your lead inspector. Your lead inspector will want to see your development planning and the SDP it is a document that your HMI/OI may request to see at the start of the inspection (there is a list of all documentation your lead inspector may ask to see, pre-inspection/on arrival, in Page 15, Paragraph 38), but whoever speaks with you in that initial phone call must not expect you to send your SDP pre-inspection. Thus the timing of the presentation of your SEF and your SDP to your lead inspector is up to you. Ofsted say that self-evaluation should not be generated solely for inspection purposes, but your self-assessment will have been updated regularly and used for different purposes, in all likelihood, anyway. What your lead inspector won't know is that you have had him, or her, in mind all the time. It would be a brave HMI who attempted to downgrade a school because they had gone against Ofsted's advice and actually prepared for their inspection! To my knowledge, it has never happened and I can't see how it ever could. However, you will be expected to show your lead inspector that you have 'an accurate understanding of your school's effectiveness' (Page 41 and 42, bullets). Indeed, aim for that phrase, or one similar, to crop up in your inspection report. If it does, you will have been successful in writing a clever, intelligent, cogent and persuasive SEF and more importantly, your school will have gained the grade you felt it deserved.

To achieve this goal of an accurate SEF, don't over-egg the pudding. If you aren't worth the grades you have put in each section of your SEF, no lead inspector is going to be persuaded by what you have written. They won't believe you. However, if you believe strongly that your school **is** worth a particular grade, but there is an ounce of possible doubt that your HMI/OI could cast doubt on that belief, especially via your most recent RAISE/ASP data, then having a persuasive SEF can tip the balance in your favour. Having supported so many schools with writing their self-evaluations and having post-inspection feedback from many other schools that have used my SEF writing dialogic tools, the weight of evidence points firmly to this being the case.

After many of those inspections, our aim was achieved and the lead inspector wrote, in the report, that the school had evaluated itself accurately. If those inspectors only knew how those schools had wrestled with their conservatism! School leaders are naturally shy about saying how good their school is. Many were initially reluctant to push for something more, even though their data showed that they were better than they thought they were. What they needed to do, in all these cases was to go for the higher of two grades, or for a split grade, and back their judgement to the hilt. I'm glad to say that's exactly what they did. If they had gone for a lower grade, I feel it is likely that a percentage of those schools would be 'Requires improvement' now, instead of 'Good' and there are others who would be 'Good' instead of being 'Outstanding'. It is far easier for a lead inspector to agree with a schools' judgement, when the school says confidently that its judgement is accurate and it backs that judgement with very persuasive and data-rich arguments, than it is to find fault with that school's judgement and downgrade the school, as a result.

The HMI, or Ofsted Inspector leading your inspection is human. They are faced with interpreting a set of criteria, each individual criterion of which is open to interpretation and is therefore subjective. This subjectivity can be used to your advantage. From these criteria, they are expected to determine a judgement that is a best fit to a grade. There are no benchmarks for what makes a school 'Good'. There are no Ofsted determinants that say a certain percentage of criteria met equals one grade, or another. Most importantly, there is nothing to say that a set of RAISE/ASP, or other data, is sufficient, or insufficient, to achieve any judgement grade. Because your lead inspector is human, they are capable of being nudged towards a desired position with the right approach and clever schools can do exactly that. Your SEF is the first step towards achieving that goal.

Your aim, in writing your SEF, is to remove as many doubts as you can from your lead inspector's mind before they sign into your school at 7.50am on the day of your inspection. An HMI/OI who is thinking along the same lines as you, will give you a far easier time on inspection, than one who enters your school doubting your self-evaluation. Don't leave it to chance that alignment between the lead inspector and your school will happen during the inspection. Influence that agreement before. Make it as impossible as you can for your lead inspector to judge you differently to your own assessment, without an enormous effort of will and skill on their part.

Ofsted say that in the Section 8 inspection handbook:

> 'The HMI will start the short inspection from the assumption that the school remains good'[15]

Help that assumption to evolve into the conclusion that you still are a 'Good' school, if you feel that your school is, indeed, still; 'Good'. Your HMI/OI has only a day to cast enough doubt on your arguments to convert and look at the RI that you really don't want. Take control of your inspection right from the word go. Produce a convincing, cogent and proud self-evaluation that has the power to persuade your lead inspector that you should have another three years (or more) to continue as a 'Good' school and to improve further.

If you are have improved, since the time of your last inspection, to be, in your view, an outstanding school, put that idea into your lead inspector's mind, pre-inspection, via your SEF, then hit them with all guns blazing on the first morning of your inspection. By lunchtime, ensure they have enough belief to call Ofsted to organise an inspection team to undertake a full Section 5 inspection, to look at G1. Then during the afternoon of your Section 8 and during your Section 5, never waver from the grading standpoint you established in your SEF.

SHOULD I PLAY SAFE, OR AIM FOR THE HIGHER OF TWO POTENTIAL GRADES?

Go for the higher, or, alternatively sow the idea in your lead inspectors's mind that you **may** be the higher grade by giving a split grade. It depends on the strength of your data. Set your stall out first. Say what grade of school you feel you are and then use every word of your SEF to back your grade. '**We believe we are a good school**', or '**We believe we are at least a good school**', or '**We now believe we are an outstanding school**' send a clear and a powerful message to a reader. You are effectively saying; 'We know our school; prove us wrong'.

---

15. www.gov.uk/government/uploads/system/uploads/attachment_data/file/547227/School_inspection_handbook-section_8.pdf

In the case of you stating; '**We believe we are at least a good school**', you are first of all precluding 'RI' by suggesting G2, and introducing the possibility of 'Outstanding'. There's nothing wrong with doing this, especially if you feel that you data sets you clearly as a good school, but there may be elements of better within that data. If your HMI then feels you are not yet an 'Outstanding' school, the monitoring letter will contain many positives that you can work with and use both in your next inspection and also with stakeholders and especially MAT representatives to show your strengths.

Such a split grade can also tilt the thinking of your lead inspector towards you and can be a subtle and clever way into helping your lead inspector to consider G1. You may get a HMI/OI who is very sympathetic to your position, especially if you are a school that takes from a challenging, disadvantaged catchment. If you see this kind of lead inspector thinking beginning to develop, play upon the difficulty that changes to the framework since the last inspection have caused you and how you're a little unsure of your current grade (can anyone be truly sure, pre-inspection?). Then push your positives even harder. If you end up G2, no one can say you didn't evaluate your school correctly, or that you didn't try hard for G1. Precluding RI sends a message of confidence. You are saying to your Section 8 HMI/OI that it's not worth them considering a grade below and you are going to say exactly why you may even be a grade above.

If, however, you feel you have improved significantly from your 'Good' position at the last inspection and you are now clearly 'Outstanding', say; '**We believe we are now an outstanding school**' and never let go from that SEF position all through your Section 8 monitoring visit. If you are sensing agreement with your SEF position – and that sense of LI agreement may come early, if your data is excellent – empathise and agree with LI terms that may suggest G1. Take any opportunity to remind your lead inspector that 'Outstanding' is a no more than a best fit in each set of grade criteria. Talk also about your confidence that you can improve even further and that 'Outstanding' is, to you, just an Ofsted station on the journey to excellence in all areas. Use phrases that will speak 'ambition' to your HMI/OI. Show that you are well aware of the existence of some schools that are far better than Ofsted 'Outstanding' and you want to be one of them.

If you feel you are a 'cusp' school, it's my opinion that you should always write your SEF to the grade above, rather than be conservative. The reason is that your (human) lead inspector will always find it easier to agree with what you have written. Disagreement is more difficult, but your lead inspector will be skilled at interpreting your data. There are no benchmarks and you have to have enough ammunition to be able to defend your position. The situation to aim for is one where you know more about what your data can say, than the person leading your inspection.

If everything points to RI, you clearly can't do any of this and don't try. '**We feel we are still a school that requires improvement, but we are moving towards good**'. If this is you, accept where you are and talk about building from your present position. Mention the green shoots of recovery that are already there and be honest about the unfortunate reasons why you feel you are in this position. RI is often down to changes in leadership, with the new leadership not yet having had the time to effect enough change. If you feel this is true, stress the recent improvements, but accept the weakness. Grade 3 is better than Grade 4, awarded because you don't know your school. In addition, a G3 report containing green shoots of progress may keep the RSC from your door for long enough so you can choose your future, rather than have it forced upon you in a process of forced Academisation.

A split grade, G3/2 is not an impossible choice, but it is harder to justify a split grade standpoint here. I don't feel you should usually do that if your inspection is a short, Section 8; you being a 'Good' school at present. The only caveat to that is if there have been significant, positive changes in leadership, leading to very recent, strong, but uneven, improvements in data. In this case, say that you acknowledge the past and the impact this had on data, but the present leadership can't be responsible for that data and is beginning to move some significant parts of it. In this case, a conversion and eventual G3 would allow you to continue an improvement agenda, with some positive report comments. It would also obviate a G4.

In these possible G3 positions, schools must foresee the possible consequences and governors have to be aware of their options. As such, while you are still a G2 school, talk to other schools and other multi-academy trusts whilst improving pupil progress within your own school. Don't leave the issue to be forced by a Section 8 lead inspector who converts your inspection to look at RI, then a Section 5 inspection team who confirm it. Determine your own future while you still have the chance to do so. Joining a trust will give you at least 2 years extra to ensure that your data is strong. It may be just what you need; a trust that allows a large element of continued independence. A 'Borg Trust' (see below), joined via a forced Academisation, won't allow continued independence, although your 'old' (quite possible, HTs and governors of such 'forced' schools) school may improve.

For someone like me who supports schools for a living, those were difficult words to write. The pressures on governing bodies to academise are huge and if recent school changes have left you vulnerable to G3, I feel you must act, even though the future with the MAT that you choose is an 'unknown unknown' that I can't help you with. You know the pressures in your own local authority and area better than I do. The demise of some local authorities have left them weak and it is difficult for them to resist the pressures from Regional Schools Commissioners, backed by the DfE.

Many multi academy trusts have provided safe havens and I work with some terrific Trusts. However, joining some trusts can feel a little like being assimilated into 'the Borg', as your school can lose much of its independence. Joining a MAT will at least give your school at least two more years in which to demonstrate improvement and you may get excellent help to do so from your new MAT. If MAT negotiations are well forward, Ofsted and the RSC will be in contact with each other and your possible imminent inspection may be delayed, although a recent parliamentary report was damning about this relationship, saying:

> 'The relationship between Ofsted and RSCs, both nationally and regionally, remains unsatisfactory'.[16]

If G3 (or G4) is a possibility at your next inspection, my advice, notwithstanding the leap into the dark that this entails, is to choose a MAT while you can, rather than wait to be pushed.

If you are thinking that your data is not looking strong enough for Grade 2, you can be sure that your LI will be thinking that too and Grade 3 is a better option than 'Special Measures' (G4). If you end up Grade 4, you will be forced to academise, with few choices. Your RSC will effectively control your future. Thus, write your SEF to a G3, strongly counteracting those G4 bullets in the handbook and stressing any areas where you may actually fulfil some G2 criteria. These will exist – there are a lot of those criterion bullets in the handbook grade descriptors – and if you can convince your HMI/OI that you are not a failing school and there are some clear areas where

---

16. www.publications.parliament.uk/pa/cm201617/cmselect/cmeduc/204/204.pdf

you are improving, or even 'Good', then 'Requires Improvement' is a far better position to be in than 'Special Measures', though both grades will put you at risk of Academisation being forced on you, I'm afraid.

You may settle happily for a G2 in a split grade, G1/G2, scenario, but I doubt you would be as happy to settle for a G3, if you have been G2 before and you are currently not sure of your grade. In this case, if the data suggests 'cusp', G2/G3, go for a clear G2, be confident that you should remain a G2 school and persuade your HMI/OI that is the case. Stress all the positives. Use the G2 lifelines that I'll refer to. Commend your green shoots of progress to your inspectors. Play on the leadership changes that now give you such excellent potential. In other words, show your lead inspector that you have capacity for future improvement, despite a recent rocky spell. If your arguments don't work, at least you tried and there's always a chance they will.

At this stage, I will, temporarily, split my narrative into primary (including infant, junior and middle schools) and secondary, to talk about 'outcomes for pupils'. There are overlaps between the two separate narratives and that requires some repetition, so please skip whichever of the parts do not apply to you, or, of course, enjoy reading both! These next sections are best read in conjunction with either the primary or the secondary SEF dialogic tools in appendices 1 and 2. The dialogic tools will talk you through how to write a self-evaluation. Chapters 2.2 to 2.7 will add some flesh to the bones of those tools.

Always have a copy of the Ofsted handbook open in your browser/at the side of you as you write and refer to apposite parts of it in your SEF.

2.2 SEF Writing: Primary Self-Evaluation

You can find my primary self-evaluation dialogic tool in appendix 1. Use that tool, in conjunction with the advice in this chapter, to write your self-evaluation. Whilst writing, have the Ofsted handbook with you and quote from it, where necessary, to illustrate your evidence for your judgement that you have achieved a grade. I won't reiterate all that is in the primary SEF tool guidance here, but I will refer to apposite parts and some parts do bear repetition.

To summarise the first part of the primary SEF writing guidance:

a. set out your 'grade stall' first of all e.g. '**We believe we are a good school**' right from the start. Be clear on this and use the rest of the SEF to support this statement.

b. set your school in an Ofsted grade **context**, then in your local context. Provide evidence of how you have translated your vision to all leaders and staff here (see Chapter 2.4: SEF Writing: The Effectiveness of Leadership and Management for more).

c. provide **information about your school**, using your last inspection report section as your template. Your lead inspector will appreciate this information and it can help them to write their post-inspection G2 letter, or S5 report;

d. show how you have met the **'key issues' from your previous inspection**.

Following this introductory part, there is no doubt that the most important section of your primary SEF is then your 'Outcomes for Pupils' section. I'll provide advice around other sections when my secondary advice re-joins my narrative, but it is upon this that I'll concentrate. Data is king and I'll offer plenty of tips as to how you can use your data to the best effect.

OUTCOMES FOR PUPILS – PRIMARY SCHOOL SEF GUIDANCE

There is a bigger focus upon the outcomes for **current** pupils in this framework. It is very clear in the grade descriptors (P56/57), so don't dwell too much on past data and concentrate more on showing accelerated progress with current pupils in all years (not just in Y6). This is very important for G1/G2 and G2/G3 'cusp' schools where recent improvements in leadership have not had a long time to embed to boost results in Y6, so the full impact of improved teaching may not yet have showed up in your previous RAISE/ASP (though it may be clear in the progress of pupils in other year groups). The handbook (Page 23, Paragraph 79) states that:

'Inspectors should consider a wide range of information. No single measure, or indicator should determine judgements.'

In other words, you can provide FFT data, NFER data, local Authority data, baseline data, internal data from a commercial package, or any other non-RAISE/ASP data to make your case. Whatever data you use must be considered by your inspectors.

Include your early years data in this section of your SEF, if you are a primary school, or an infant school. It sits better here than in your early years section and you can link to other data more easily. Now for a very important statement…

> *'Skills on entry' to early years (EY) is the most crucial piece of data that any primary school can present to Ofsted.*

I've emboldened that sentence for emphasis, as it is so important. From this, progress across the whole school is judged. I've stressed the importance of skills on entry before and I make no apology for doing so again. Be conservative in assessing your children's skills to ensure progress is clear across YN and YR. Also ensure that your lead inspector does not get carried away by RAISE/ASP data around skills on entry to Reception if your own Nursery has contributed the bulk of that. Explain this carefully in your SEF.

On leaving YR, ensure that assessments of whether children have achieved a good level of development (GLD) are not so positive as to put undue pressure on your measures of progress across KS1. You are in charge of both assessing skills on entry and assessing GLD. YOU are also in charge of any baseline assessments you may have done (baseline assessment is 'on hold' at the time of writing!) are all are subjective. You are the main arbiter here. Schools do disagree with local authority moderations. However, don't assess wrongly simply to aggrandise EY progress. It will be clear to inspectors if your pupils are much more capable than you are saying, but it would take a current early years specialist to argue with you on points of EYFSP assessment and they generally not HMI.

Just don't create a progression profile through early years that either shows that children make slow progress in YN, or YR, or that they make so much progress that Key Stage 1 appears not to build well on the high numbers of children with a good level of development. I must stress that nothing changes for the pupils. They make the same progress from entry to the end of KS1, but a lack of cleverness can leave you presenting a weak Key Stage 1, or weaknesses in early years, to your HMI/OI and that could be disastrous. All these assessments are in your hands, so **be sensible**. Your previous lead inspector's assessment of children's skills on entry, as described in your last inspection report, can be used as a guide. Their assessment of EY skills on entry, will certainly be used, this time, as a guide by your lead inspector.

If you are an infant school and especially if you have a deprived catchment, then a very careful establishment of children's skills on entry to your school is vital. Be as conservative as you can with your initial skills assessment. If you have no Nursery, you have only three years in which to demonstrate progress to your inspectors and if your exit data is still showing attainment below national norms, the only way to demonstrate progress is by talking about progress from very low skills on entry. In this situation, progress to KS1 outcomes below national can still represent excellent progress, if handled well. Again, use the description of skills on entry from your last inspection report as a guide, though these may have declined over the intervening period. I have no hesitation in repeating handbook information around judging progress just for you. The handbook (Page 53, Paragraph 75) is very clear to inspectors that they must give most weight to pupils' progress and to pupils currently in the school. They must also consider the progress of all year groups:

> 'In judging achievement, inspectors will give most weight to pupils' progress. They will take account of pupils' starting points in terms of their prior attainment and age when evaluating progress. Within this, they will give most weight to the progress of pupils currently in the school, taking account of how this compares with the progress of recent cohorts, where there are any. Inspectors will consider the progress of pupils in all year groups, not just those who have taken or are about to take examinations or national tests. As part of pupils' progress, inspectors will consider the growth in pupils' security, breadth and depth of knowledge, understanding and skills.'

Hopefully your HMI/OI will understand how to determine progress across an infant school, but in this situation, if your HMI/OI wants to concentrate on RAISE/ASP and your data dashboard, all they are likely to see are poor comparisons to national attainment norms, if your catchment is deprived. There's a situation where you simply must be clued in, as to what to do. If your lead inspector wishes to focus on RAISE/ASP attainment data and RAISE/ASP data alone, an infant school has to complain and complain immediately. I raise the spectre of complaints a little later in the book!

DATA AND ESPECIALLY PROGRESS IS KING

Let's have a look at some of the things that can affect progress measures in primary schools and how you may be able to use them to convince an HMI that your progress may not be quite as shown in RAISE/ASP.

There is currently no aggregate progress measure at KS1, like there is at KS2. Instead there is a fairly crude proxy of how many pupils fail and reach 'expected levels, or above' and are working at 'greater depth' from their Early years Foundation Stage Profile early learning goals data from two years before (i.e. whether they were emerging, expected, exceeding). This is also expressed as a percentage. Breaking the cohort down into these areas can leave small numbers in each group. Page 23, Paragraph 80 of the handbook cautions inspectors in dealing with small numbers:

'Inspectors should not report separately on small numbers (typically fewer than five) where individual pupils could be identified.'

This advice applies to using RAISE/ASP data in all Key Stages. As well as the handbook warning, at training, OIs and HMIs were always cautioned about drawing firm conclusions from data cohorts of fewer than 10 pupils. Caution your lead inspector in the same way, if they are beginning to draw conclusions from cohorts of between 5 and 10 pupils. For example, if your HMI wishes to draw conclusions from only a few disadvantaged pupils whose GLD showed they were higher attainers (exceeding) at the start of KS1, gently remind them of their training. If you have the data, point to the progress of higher attaining disadvantaged pupils in the current year 6 and in other year groups, for balance.

At KS2, there is an progress aggregate measure which is calculated from the levels the pupils achieved at KS1, to the scaled scores achieved at KS2 across all their subjects except for writing, where attainment is teacher assessed. Technical information about this calculation for 2016 can be found at:

www.gov.uk/government/uploads/system/uploads/attachment_data/
file/583768/primary_school_accountability_technical_guidance_January_17.pdf

The measure itself has critics, however RAISE/ASP saddles you with a progress score.
That saddle may rest easily on a school with good progress data, but may not in
schools with weaker data, or schools who draw from more deprived catchments. The
next section applies to G2/3 cusp schools, as well as to schools with very negative
progress scores. There are three things schools can analyse further and all three
could provide a persuasive lifeline to the grade you want.

POSSIBLE G2 LIFELINES FOR A PRIMARY SCHOOL
a) Explain the progress of your current pupils fully

The August 2015 framework and handbook changes and all subsequent versions
of the handbook, included an increased emphasis on the **progress of current
pupils**. Reflect this by including data for pupil progress to date in the current year
leading up to inspection, by whatever means you use to track progress. This could be
a commercial package and that's OK, as inspectors must look at all data presented.
A short explanation of how you show and use progress data may be helpful to your
lead inspector, as they may not have come across your particular assessment system
before.

You could be showing poor data up to the previous RAISE/ASP report and in
consequence, your Inspection Dashboard will be very negative. However, leadership
and teaching could have been already improving, but this improvement had not
yet enough time to take full effect by the time of the publication of your last report.
In this case, this could be a lifeline to G2. Data may not be just improving in the
current Y6 and the current Y2, but improvements may be clear in other year groups,
and progress may already have been accelerating in those year groups during the
previous year. Talk about these legacy issues in your SEF, if the leadership team is
newer and progress has been historically weak, but is now accelerating.

None of this will have been seen in last year's RAISE/ASP, of course. Stress these
unseen (to your inspectors through the data they are given, pre-inspection) progress
improvements and clearly explain the links to improving quality of leadership and
teaching improvements. Pro-forma tables could be prepared that can easily be
updated straight after the inspection phone call with your latest data drop. If you
can persuade your inspection team that a corner has already been turned in pupil

progress, you may have a vital way in to persuading your lead inspector that your school is improving, or that last year's Y6 and Y2 data are not the start of a declining trend. Thus you can help them to develop an idea that it would be best to leave you alone for at least another 3 years, as a school that continues to be 'Good'.

b) Transience (stability)

Be very clear on how transience, both into and out of a cohort through a Key Stage may have affected your data. Next to explaining your attainment on entry to KS2 (junior schools especially), high transience can be the key to explaining why attainment outcomes may not be showing correctly in RAISE/ASP. It may just provide you with a G2 lifeline.

Be sure of which pupils bring data with them and which pupils don't. If a pupil joins in Y6 but completed KS1 at a different school (which may not be their last school) their progress is calculated to their scaled score with you, from their KS1 score at another school. P23 of the 'Primary school accountability in 2016 – A technical guide for primary maintained schools, academies and free schools' says:

> 'Where pupils have moved schools between key stage 1 and key stage 2, we will retrieve their key stage 1 data and include them in the progress calculation for their current school.'[17]

This means that you may be responsible for the progress of a pupil who only spent a small proportion of their KS2 with you. Such pupils always have stories and if this pupil was PP/SEND and had been a poor attender before coming to you, you could end up responsible for a negative progress outlier, which could skew your results. This is especially true for smaller primaries.

Your transients may well have made good progress in the short time they have been in your care, but you haven't had them for a full Key Stage. They have not had the full experience of your school and you cannot be responsible for a pupil's poor progress in another school. This is madness on the part of RAISE/ASP and you should not be hung for it on Ofsted. Disaggregate these pupils and re-calculate your progress and attainment scores, explaining the reasons to your HMI/OI, through your SEF.

---

17. www.gov.uk/government/uploads/system/uploads/attachment_data/file/583768/primary_school_accountability_technical_guidance_January_17.pdf

At least RAISE/ASP **may** allow you to remove some pupils, especially those who recently came from abroad (P24 of 'Primary school accountability in 2016'):

> 'In limited circumstances, schools may request that a pupil be omitted from performance measures, for example, if pupils have recently arrived from overseas'.

Be aware that your % stability measure in RAISE/ASP is whole-school stability and does not indicate transience in particular year groups, which may vary a great deal. If transience in your last Y6/Y2 cohort was higher than usual, my advice is to disaggregate your transient pupils for your Y6 (and possibly, Y2 cohorts) and recalculate your attainment and progress data without them. Tabulate this alongside your RAISE/ASP data. The results could be illuminating and your inspectors must 'consider' all data presented by you (Page 23, Paragraph 79). However, if it doesn't help you; don't present it!

> 'During inspection, inspectors should consider performance information presented by the school for current pupils across year groups and previous cohorts, including that provided by external organisations. They should also consider the published data available to them before the inspection.'

And yet again, Paragraph 77, further down the same page is worth repeating:

> 'Inspectors should consider a wide range of information. No single measure or indicator should determine judgements.'

An example here to illustrate where RAISEonline was badly wrong. I led the inspection of a primary school, almost surrounded by an army base, some years ago. Almost all their pupils were therefore transients, as their parents moved often and did tours abroad. The average length of stay of pupils was about two years. The data showed blue across the board and when I first looked at the school's data, it was a sucking-of-air-through-my-teeth moment, as it looked horrendous. All I thought was G4. However, you never know what you'll find when you walk through the door of a school and within ten minutes and with 95% transience, we effectively took RAISE and placed it in the bin. The school was quite wonderful and what they were doing with kids, many of whom came from some very challenging backgrounds was nothing short of remarkable. This was an 'Outstanding' school, with, potentially, 'Special Measures' RAISE data. RAISE and its successor, ASP do not tell the whole story!

Don't forget the pupils who left during KS2. These may have been of high ability, or had progressed, in your care, to pupils who were working at a high level. They would have benefitted your attainment results, had they stayed. If you have higher than average transience, I'm sure you have had examples of some very bright 'level 3' pupils who left to join another school just before SATs! RAISE/ASP is happy to attribute to you the KS1 scores of pupils who didn't join at the start of KS2, so don't be afraid, in return, to speculate on the attainment you've lost out on, due to higher ability pupils leaving late in KS2. Same caveat: if the results don't benefit you, don't present them to your HMI.

c) Outliers

By outliers, I mean the lowest performing pupils in your attainment and progress RAISE/ASP scatterplots on P20-29 of 2016 RAISE/ASP. These pupils are lower and well detached from the main body of your students on those graphs. The effects of outliers can be a possible third G2 lifeline. I've begun to allude to this above. I hope your HMI/OI understands the effect that outliers – which could lie beyond your control – could have on your progress and your attainment data. If they don't, you must be able to explain!

These outliers will all have a story. Pupils underperform for reasons. Present a spreadsheet showing each of your outliers and the story behind their lower than expected performance. SEND, EAL, disadvantage and/or vulnerability are often involved, together with transience and these factors may overlap. It is important to get to pupil level on these outliers, as you may be talking about a small number of pupils, who had outrageous outliers, that, in a small primary especially, could totally skew your data. Even in a larger primary, the effect of a few extreme outliers can have an inordinate effect on what would have been good progress and attainment data.

Jamie Pembroke (@jpembroke on Twitter and very well worth following) highlighted another issue with outliers for me via a direct message:

> 'The current KS2 VA methodology means outliers are inevitable. The issue centres on pre-key stage pupils and nominal scores. VA estimates for low prior attaining (PA) SEND pupils are too high due to high progress rates of low PA EAL pupils. SEND and EAL pupils with low PA treated the same and have same benchmarks. The nominal scoring system therefore gives rise to negative VA scores as low as -25. This makes me mad when accountability

guidance states progress measure will reflect progress made by all pupils. Nonsense!'

In this example, every other pupil in a class of 25 would have to gain at least +1.0 in their progress measure to compensate for that one extreme outlier. If you had a pupil, in a class of 25, whose progress score was -5, they will have reduced the overall cohort's progress score by 0.2.'

It is well worth getting to the bottom of why you have outliers (if indeed you do) and explaining the performance of those particularly low-performing pupils in detail. Know your stuff here. Know it better than your lead inspector will. Know it so well you can teach that lead inspector – always the best position for a teacher to be in!

All this advice about possible lifelines will enable you and your leaders to talk about the progress of your pupils in depth and your knowledge may then exceed that of your HMI. That's a more comfortable position to be in, than finding out, on inspection, that your HMI knows more than you do about what your own data shows. You can bet your life that they won't reveal these possible unknowns of the progress of current pupils, transients and outliers to you on inspection, if you are not a clearly good school. That's not, ostensibly, what inspection is about. It is a judgmental process, but your lead inspector is human and his/her work has to fit a framework and Ofsted's report writing expectations.

Your lead inspector/HMI has to ensure they can get their grade through quality assurance. They will work with you to show your data in the best possible light only if they need to get your data to fit their grade. If your lead inspector and their team feel you are a 'Good' school, but there is data that doesn't, on the surface, support a grade of 'Good', they will shape your data so it reflects 'Good' criteria in the handbook. This could involve using the three 'lifeline' possibilities highlighted above, discussing them in detail with you and working with you to ensure that the finished 'outcomes for pupils' evidence fits the 'outcomes for pupils' criteria. However, if your HMI becomes convinced you are G3, or G4, they'll still be working to get your data to fit their grade – but that won't be a help to you. Those 'lifelines' are very unlikely to be mentioned. Remember: the inspection process is subjective. Every decision of your lead inspector and the inspection team is subjective. Glass half-full/glass half-empty?

Thus, be prepared via your self-evaluation. Don't leave your outcome to chance on the day.

If you are a junior school then, for me, you are the biggest case in point for understanding your data extremely well. You must carefully construct a case for good pupil progress, as you are not responsible for any of the data that your pupils bring with them from KS1.

Progress across your school is simply KS2 RAISE/ASP progress data and there is no other measure of progress for your school that your HMI will see prior to receiving your SEF. Your on-entry data is the exit data from your Infant school(s) and if I were an Infant school headteacher, I'd want to make damn sure that my teacher assessments at KS1 showed my school in the best possible light. Thus, junior schools often feel they are hamstrung by the on-entry data from their, often neighbouring, infant school(s).

Why have previous LA education regimes and governments allowed this infant/junior division to perpetuate? I've supported several sets of infant and junior schools that are separated only by a wall – and in one case, a shared school field – who were so far apart on the assessment of their pupils that they could almost be in different continents. So which data does an inspector believe?

If you are a junior school, or an infant school, follow the advice contained in 'Taking Control' and fight your own corner from that advice. I know of instances where both, separate, infant and junior schools have been judged to be 'Good' as both were very persuasive about their data to their respective and different, inspection teams, yet data overall from YR to Y6, might have put a combined school as no better than 'Requires Improvement'. Crazy, but true!

As a result, junior schools should consider re-basing their on-entry data, perhaps using testing, such as National Foundation for Educational Research (NFER) tests, to determine their own baseline for Y3 pupils joining their school. If you don't do this and you accept your RAISE/ASP on-entry data as correct, your pupils may have to make superhuman progress to even appear to get to the national progress norm of 0.0. There's unfairness in this system that often can only be resolved by school amalgamation. Any junior school or infant headteacher who reads this will understand.

A junior school should present re-baselined data alongside its RAISE/ASP data, then build a cogent supporting argument via:

- the evidence you've seen of pupils' starting points in their early work in Y3 books;
- the progress you see overall in individual year groups;
- the progress you see in the books of pupils in all other year groups.

In addition, do the same analyses around transient pupils and outliers, as I've detailed above. Remember that the progress of your current pupils is paramount, so be prepared to drop your most recent progress data straight into your RAISE/ASP, immediately following your initial phone call with your lead inspector.

Effectively, if you feel your feeder infant schools over-assess your pupils at the end of Y2, you have to make the case that RAISE/ASP progress scores may well be skewed negatively by that data and therefore RAISE/ASP does not paint an accurate picture of progress in your school. RAISE/ASP is therefore wrong. Experience tells me that this argument that you can win.

If you are a middle school. Your arguments to your inspectors are similar to those of junior schools, but you mustn't let RAISE/ASP Y6 outcome data dominate your inspection. Nail your attainment on entry, first and foremost. Baseline your pupils carefully and evidence their attainment when they leave just as thoroughly. Use your own, or other commercial products to measure pupil progress across your school, their attainment when the pupils leave and their progress within year groups. Remember, inspectors must look at all evidence presented to them.

Don't allow your HMI/OI to focus solely upon RAISE/ASP. They shouldn't anyway, as none of your pupils started KS2, so therefore any RAISE/ASP progress measure to Y6 is effectively worth nothing. You are in control of the progress baseline, as you should be in control of showing the progress of your pupils to when they leave. Pupil progress is always measured from pupils' starting points to when they leave your school, so the same advice applies for transient pupils, as it does for other schools. Disaggregate your transients and recalculate any data, presenting it alongside RAISE/ASP data for Y6 and the same for attainment on leaving. Progress of current pupils is still paramount, but you have many ways of taking control of your data. Prepare your data arguments well, but look upon your unique position, with pupils not leaving at the end of a RAISE/ASP-reported key stage, as a big, positive, lever to your inspection grade!

EARLY YEARS (EY)

Early years are given a separate grade on inspection, with separate judgement criteria. Thus there is a whole separate section in the handbook devoted to this (Page 58): *'Inspecting the effectiveness of the early years provision: quality and standards'*. All the other major areas of school inspection are also inspected in early years. Inspectors will examine the effectiveness of leadership and management in early years, the quality of teaching in early years, the personal development behaviour and welfare of pupils in early years and outcomes for pupils in early years. There are no numerical grades given, if your inspection is a Section 5 inspection, but instead, grades will be implicit, or even explicit, in the writing. For example, this kind of phrase may be used as an opener, then each separate area will be included in subsequent bullet points; 'Leaders in the early years reflect the high standards and expectations seen across the whole school'.

Thus, in your self-evaluation, write early years as a series of sub-headings, for each of the major areas that will be inspected. Apply all the advice contained in the separate self-evaluation chapters in *'Taking Control'*. When writing your 'outcomes for pupils' section, however, don't repeat all of the data contained in your main school 'outcomes for pupils' section. Instead, refer briefly to this data and repeat your overall conclusions about the entry, exit and progress data of children in early years.

2.3 SEF Writing: Secondary Self-Evaluation

You can find my secondary self-evaluation dialogic tool in appendix 2. Use that tool, in conjunction with the advice in this chapter, to write your self-evaluation. Whilst writing, have the Ofsted handbook with you and quote from it, where necessary, to illustrate your evidence for your judgement that you have achieved a particular grade. I won't reiterate all that is in the secondary SEF tool guidance here, but I will refer to apposite parts and some parts do bear repetition.

To summarise the first part of the secondary SEF writing guidance:

a. set out your 'grade stall' first of all e.g. '**We believe we are a good school**' right from the start. Be clear on this and use the rest of the SEF to support this statement;

b. set your school in an Ofsted grade context, then in your local context;

c. provide information about your school, using your last inspection report section as your template. Your LI will appreciate this information and it can help them to write their post-inspection G2 letter, or S5 report;

d. show how you have met the 'key issues' from your previous inspection.

Following this introductory part, there is no doubt that the most important section of your secondary SEF is then your 'Outcomes for Pupils' section. I'll provide advice around other sections when my primary narrative re-joins, but it is upon 'Outcomes for Pupils' that I'll concentrate here. Data is king and I'll offer plenty of tips as to how you can use your data to the best effect. Separate your sixth form data though. The sixth form, per se, is not judged on inspection, but 'the effectiveness of the 16-19 study programmes' is. Data here does not overlap, or continue in a linear way from GCSE data, being assessed very differently, so 16-19 data can sit in your 16-19 section and not your 'outcomes for pupils' section.

OUTCOMES FOR PUPILS – SECONDARY SCHOOL SEF GUIDANCE

There is a bigger focus upon the outcomes for **current** pupils in this framework. This is very clear in the grade descriptors (Page 56 and 57), so don't dwell too much on past data and concentrate more on showing accelerated progress with current pupils in all years (not just in Y11). This is very important for G1/G2 and G2/G3 'cusp' schools where recent improvements in leadership have not had a long time to embed to boost results in Y11, or in the sixth form, so the impact of improved teaching may not yet have showed up in your previous RAISE/ASP (though it may be clear in the progress of pupils in other year groups). The handbook (Page 23, Paragraph 79) states that:

> 'Inspectors should consider a wide range of information. No single measure, or indicator should determine judgements.'

In other words, you can provide FFT data, NFER test data, local Authority data, baseline data, ALIS data, YELLIS data, internal data from a commercial package, or any other non-RAISE/ASP data to make your case.

We must remember that **data and especially progress data is king**, so let us look at how this could be used to back an assertion that, despite, at face value, less than perfect RAISE/ASP data, pupils in your school are making good progress.

Before we do this, let me state, again, that 'Taking Control' can't save you, if your school is not doing a good enough job for your pupils and they really aren't making expected progress. In that case, G3, or G4, will be a deserved inspection outcome, as may be the consequences. Above everything else –and we may not like this – apart from the expectation that pupils are kept safe, inspection demands primarily that secondary pupils make academic progress, no matter what we may feel about the education of the whole child.

1. IS YOUR ATTAINMENT ON ENTRY TO Y7 ACCURATE?
It is possible to argue that assessment by your feeder primaries is not accurate. Primaries often do a brilliant job in preparing their pupils well for SATs (Standard Assessment Tests). The pupils reach peak exam performance for those SATs in May of Y6, but the results achieved may not reflect the actual abilities of the pupils. They may reflect, to some extent, some excellent preparation, by their teachers, for the pupils' SATs. This can be especially true in writing, where primary assessment is by teachers and not via a standardised test, but even in mathematics and reading, pupils may have been very well coached, even tutored, to pass their SATs. Approaches will also differ between your feeder primary schools, so their SATs results may not properly reflect their ability in the subject. This SAT-readiness thus may not reflect their true abilities at 11 years old.

The Y7 'dip' is well documented but the achievement of pupils prior to the 'dip' can create a false starting point for your particular pupils and put your early KS3 progress results under pressure, if not your progress measures across the whole school. Your inspectors may feel that 5 years may be considered long enough for you to have redressed any potential over-assessment, or targeted SATs exam preparation, but that does not change the fact that it may be there in your prior attainment data and therefore your Y11 RAISE/ASP progress data, so argue your case if you feel it necessary that RAISE/ASP on-entry data for your school may not be accurate.

Some schools accept their pupils' prior attainment from KS2 and move on. If that is the case and RAISE/ASP shows that your pupils make good progress from Y7 to GCSE, then well done and this next section may not be for you. If your pupils don't appear to make the progress in published results, equivalent to that that you feel you often see in your classrooms, consider re-baselining your pupils, using CATs scores, NFER tests, or any other means you can, to cast doubt on RAISE/ASP prior attainment scores. RAISE/ASP gives a far from perfect assessment of the progress of your pupils to GCSE. RAISE/ASP data is not the be-all and end-all of how you can demonstrate that the vast majority of your pupils have made progress, as we will see.

Your previous lead inspector's assessment of children's skills on entry, as described in your last inspection report, can be used as a guide. That assessment will certainly be used as a guide by your lead inspector. However, there may have been changes since your last report in the abilities of your Y7 cohorts. Your catchment demographics may be changing. This can have an influence on pre-GCSE cohorts and their progress from their starting points and explain this through your SEF.

The handbook (Page 53, Paragraph 75) is very clear to inspectors that they must give most weight to pupils' progress and to pupils currently in the school, they must examine pupils starting points and they must examine all data provided by the school. They must also consider the progress of all year groups:

> 'In judging achievement, inspectors will give most weight to pupils' progress.
> They will take account of pupils' starting points in terms of their prior
> attainment and age when evaluating progress. Within this, they will give
> most weight to the progress of pupils currently in the school, taking account
> of how this compares with the progress of recent cohorts, where there are
> any. Inspectors will consider the progress of pupils in all year groups, not just

those who have taken or are about to take examinations or national tests. As part of pupils' progress, inspectors will consider the growth in pupils' security, breadth and depth of knowledge, understanding and skills.'

Thus a thorough examination of whether RAISE/ASP paints an accurate picture of your pupils' starting points is worthwhile. If you find that RAISE/ASP prior performance data doesn't show your pupils' joining abilities accurately, consider re-basing your pupils, using the Cognitive Abilities Tests (CAT4, run by GL Education Group Ltd.), or any other tests to determine ability for individual subjects, to determine your own baseline for the Y7 pupils joining your school. If you don't do this and you accept your RAISE/ASP on-entry data as correct, your pupils may have to make superhuman progress to appear to get to the national progress 8 expected value of 0.0, never mind make greater than expected progress.

A secondary school can present re-baselined data alongside its RAISE/ASP data, then build a cogent supporting argument via:

- the evidence you've seen of pupils' starting points in their early work in Y3 books;
- the progress you see overall in other year groups;
- the progress you see in the books of pupils in all other year groups.

In addition, do the same analyses around transient pupils and outliers, as I detail in 'Possible G2 lifelines for a secondary school' below. Remember that the progress of your current pupils is paramount, so be prepared to drop your most recent progress data straight into your RAISE/ASP, immediately following your initial phone call with your lead inspector.

Effectively, if you feel your feeder primary schools over-assess your pupils at the end of Y2, you have to make the case that RAISE/ASP progress scores may well be skewed negatively by the data and therefore RAISE/ASP does not paint an accurate picture of progress in your school. RAISE/ASP is therefore wrong. As I've said already, experience tells me that this argument that you can win.

DATA AND ESPECIALLY PROGRESS DATA IS KING
Having examined the veracity of your RAISE/ASP attainment on-entry data, let's have a look at some of the things that can affect progress measures in secondary schools

and how you may be able to use them to convince an HMI that your progress may not be quite as shown in the headline figures in RAISE/ASP.

The main progress measure at GCSE is Progress 8 (P8) and the leadership of every secondary school knows the make-up of the measure in great detail. Further information as to how it is calculated can be found here via the DfE[18] or via RAISE.[19]

Many other organisations, including NAHT, SISRA, PIXL and Education Datalab provide their own analyses of GCSE data and especially progress, outside of RAISE/ASP.

SMALL NUMBERS IN RAISE/ASP P8 GROUPS

Firstly, because RAISE/ASP breaks down progress data into the progress of, sometimes, very small groups of pupils; bear this Ofsted handbook advice in mind when analysing your data (Page 23, Paragraph 80):

> 'Inspectors should not report separately on small numbers (typically fewer than five) – but, thus, not always fewer than five – where individual pupils could be identified.' (My insertion)

This advice applies to using RAISE/ASP data in all Key Stages. As well as the handbook warning about interpreting the data of small numbers of pupils, at training, OIs and HMIs were always cautioned about drawing firm conclusions from data cohorts of fewer than 10 pupils. Caution your lead inspector in the same way, if they are beginning to draw conclusions from cohorts of between 5 and 10 pupils. For example, if your HMI wishes to draw conclusions from only a few disadvantaged pupils whose progress showed they were higher attainers at the start of KS3 (a current Ofsted hot topic), gently remind them of their training. In addition and if you have the data, point to the progress of higher attaining disadvantaged pupils in the current year 11, in other year groups and in previous years, for balance.

The Progress 8 measure itself has many critics, however, RAISE/ASP saddles you with a progress score where every pupil, regardless of disadvantage, is compared to every other pupil. That saddle may rest easily on a school with good progress data, but the next section applies to G2/3 cusp schools, as well as to schools with very

---

18. www.gov.uk/government/publications/progress-8-school-performance-measure
19. www.raiseonline.org/OpenDocument.aspx?document=392

negative progress scores. There are three things schools can analyse further and all three could provide a persuasive lifeline to the grade you want:

POSSIBLE G2 LIFELINES FOR A SECONDARY SCHOOL
a) Explain the progress of your current pupils fully
The August 2015 framework and handbook changes and all subsequent versions of the handbook, included an increased emphasis on the **progress of current pupils**. Reflect this by including data for pupil progress to date in the current year leading up to inspection, by whatever means you use to track progress. This could be a commercial package and that's OK, as inspectors must look at all data presented. A short explanation of how you show and use progress data may be helpful to your lead inspector, as they may not have come across it before.

If you are showing, at face value, weaker data up to the previous RAISE/ASP report (and Inspection Dashboard), however, leadership and teaching were already improving, but had not yet had enough time to take full effect by the time of the publication of your data, this could be a lifeline to G2. Data may not be just improving in the current Y11, but improvements may be clear in other year groups. Indeed, progress may already have been accelerating in those year groups during the previous year, but this will not be reported in RAISE/ASP. If this is the case, talk about leadership and management legacy issues in your SEF, the leadership team is new and progress has been historically weak under an old leadership regime, but is now accelerating. Also, talk about curriculum legacy issues, if the leadership team has inherited them. Changes in early entry requirements and in which subjects qualify for progress 8 'pots' have led to some schools suffering badly from those changes. These are working their way through school results, but if you are still suffering, this is a cogent argument to present and to re-calculate your P8 without your negative legacies.

None of this will have been seen by your lead inspector in RAISE/ASP in the pre-inspection information they are given. Stress these unseen (by your LI) progress improvements and explain the links to improved quality of leadership and teaching improvements, very clearly. Pro-forma tables can be prepared that can easily be updated straight after the inspection phone call with your latest data drop. If you can persuade your inspection team that a corner has already been turned in pupil progress, you may have a vital way in to persuading your lead inspector that your school is improving, or that last year's Y11 data is not the start of a declining trend.

Thus you can help them to develop an idea that they can leave you alone for at least another 3 years, as a school that continues to be 'Good'.

b) Transience (stability)

Be very clear on how transience, both into and out of a cohort through a Key Stage may have affected your data. A strong explanation of your (possibly) high transience can be another key to explaining why attainment outcomes may not be showing correctly in RAISE/ASP. It may just provide you with a G2 lifeline.

Also be sure of which pupils bring data with them and which pupils don't. If a pupil joins in Y11 but completed Yrs 7-10 at a different school (which may not be their only secondary school, of course) their KS2 data follows them. Thus progress is calculated to GCSE from Y7, as if they had been with you. P23 of the 'Progress 8 and Attainment 8 Guide for maintained secondary schools, academies and free schools' says:

> 'Where pupils have moved schools between key stage 1 and key stage 2, we will retrieve their key stage 1 data and include them in the progress calculation for their current school.'[20]

This means that you may be responsible for the progress of a pupil who only spent a small proportion of their KS2 with you. Such pupils always have stories and if this pupil was PP/SEND and had been a poor attender before coming to you, you could end up responsible for a negative progress outlier that could skew your results. This is especially true for smaller secondaries.

Your transients may well have made good progress in the short time they have been in your care, but they have not had the full experience of your school and you cannot be responsible for a pupil's poor progress in another school. This is madness on the part of RAISE/ASP and you should not be hung for it on Ofsted. Disaggregate these pupils and re-calculate your progress and attainment scores, explaining the reasons to your HMI/OI, through your SEF.

At least RAISE/ASP does allow you to remove any pupils who recently came from abroad (again P23 of the 'Progress 8 and Attainment 8 Guide for maintained secondary schools, academies and free schools'):

20. www.gov.uk/government/uploads/system/uploads/attachment_data/file/583768/primary_ school_accountability_technical_guidance_January_17.pdf

'In limited circumstances, schools may request that a pupil be omitted from performance measures, for example, if pupils have recently arrived from overseas'.

Be aware that your % stability measure in RAISE/ASP is whole-school stability and does not indicate transience in particular year groups, which may vary a great deal. If transience in your last Y11 cohort was higher than usual, my advice is to disaggregate your transient pupils from this cohort and recalculate your attainment and progress data without them. This is especially true for pupils who joined late. Tabulate this alongside your RAISE/ASP data. The results could be illuminating to your inspectors, as it may demonstrate what your school can do, given that pupils stay for a full five years. Inspectors must 'consider' all data (termed 'performance information' by Ofsted, recently). However, if it doesn't help you; don't present it! The Ofsted handbook (Page 23, Paragraph 79) says:

'During inspection, inspectors should consider performance information presented by the school for current pupils across year groups and previous cohorts, including that provided by external organisations. They should also consider the published data available to them before the inspection.'

And yet again (Paragraph 77) further down the same page is worth repeating:

'Inspectors should consider a wide range of information. No single measure or indicator should determine judgements.'

Don't forget the pupils who left during KS3/4. These pupils may have been, on average, of higher ability than the cohort left behind and may have benefitted your attainment results, had they stayed and achieved the average progress of the rest of that cohort. They may also have the effect of effectively depressing your cohort attainment's ability – seen in your attainment on entry table on P56 of 2016 RAISE/ASP – as they moved through from Y7 to Y11. This can be the case if your school is in a catchment with have a grammar, or private school close by and parents move their pupils for GCSE. If this is the case, it should be explained carefully in your SEF. Also, if you have higher than average transience, I'm sure you have had examples of some very bright 'level 5' pupils who left to join another school just before the start of KS4. RAISE/ASP is happy to attribute to you the KS2 scores of pupils who didn't join you at the start of Y7, so don't be afraid, in return, to speculate on the attainment you've lost out on, due to higher ability pupils leaving late in KS3, or in KS4 – especially if your higher ability pupils do well. Same caveat: if the results don't benefit you, don't present them to your HMI.

c) Outliers

By outliers, I mean the lowest performing pupils in your attainment and progress RAISE/ASP scatterplots. These pupils are the ones well detached from the main body of your students on those graphs. The effects of those outliers can be a possible third G2 lifeline. I've begun to allude to this above. I hope your HMI/OI understands the effect that outliers – which could lie beyond your control – may have on your progress and your attainment data. If they don't, you must be able to explain!

These outliers will all have a story. Pupils underperform for reasons. Present a spreadsheet showing each of your outlier pupils and the story behind their lower than expected performance. SEND, EAL, disadvantage and/or vulnerability are often involved, together with transience and these factors often overlap. It is important to get to pupil level on these outliers, as you may be talking about a small number of pupils, who had outrageous outliers, that, in a smaller secondary especially, could skew your data negatively. Even in a larger secondary, the effect of some extreme outliers can have an inordinate effect on your progress and attainment data.

Progress 8 is an inadequate average measure – massively open to distortion by outliers.

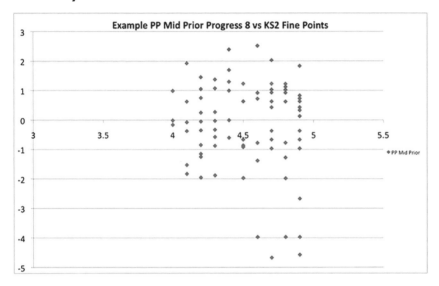

These 80 Middle attaining PP students have P8 = -0.20;
without the 5 obvious outliers, P8 = +0.07.

Take the sample data above. This is based on real school data via a Headteacher colleague but the figures and details are changed. On face value, P8 for this sub-group of 80 students is -0.20. That's certainly below average with a degree of significance. A report might state: Middle Ability Disadvantaged students make below average progress based on this data. But, actually that's not quite true. It only takes five students out of 80 in the group to distort the average. These five students each have very low P8 scores – signifying major issues with final exams. Any number of factors could be at play but they wouldn't be related to standards as such; at this scale it would need to be missed exams, massive exam blow-outs and so on. Outliers 'lie outside' the main pattern of a data set. It's fair to say that these five students don't represent general standards or issues for this group. 75 out of 80 students – those that constitute the core group of this sub-group – actually score P8 +0.07. It's not even negative. The crude, raw average doesn't really tell the story of achievement for the group – unless it is broken down and explored.

Clearly outcomes for those five students matter – but their numerical attainment scores have an undue effect on what is an arbitrary numerical representation of 'progress and standards' and this needs to be recognised if we're going to talk sensibly about these things in the context of school improvement.'[21] *(Tom Sherrington)*

It is well worth getting to the bottom of why you have outliers (if indeed you do) and explaining the performance of those particularly low-performing pupils in detail. Know your stuff here. Know it better than your lead inspector will. Know it so well you can teach your lead inspector – always the best position to be in!

All this advice about possible lifelines will enable you and your leaders to talk about the progress of your pupils in depth. Your knowledge may then exceed that of your HMI. As I've said, that's a good position to be in and much more comfortable than finding out, on inspection, that your HMI knows more than you do about what he/she thinks your own data shows. You can bet your life that they won't reveal these four possible unknowns of: flawed attainment of entry, the progress of current pupils, transients and outliers, to you on inspection, if you are not a clearly good school. Helping schools to a higher grade is not what inspection is about and though I agree with Ofsted's mantra for HMI's of 'do good as you go', the mantra does not stretch as far as this! In the end, inspection is a judgmental process and your, very human, LI has to write a report and ensure an evidence base, that fits a framework and Ofsted's report writing expectations. They are not going to give you these clues for a potential G2, if they are feeling that your school is a G3. I'll repeat: every judgement your LI makes is subjective and inspectors can be swayed by cogent arguments around data.

Your lead inspector/HMI has to ensure they can get their grade through quality assurance. They will work with you to show your data in the best possible light only if they need to get your data to fit a higher grade. If your lead inspector and their team feel you are a 'Good' school, but there is data that doesn't, on the surface, support a grade of 'Good', they will help you to shape your data so that it reflects the 'Good' criteria in the handbook. This could involve using the three 'lifeline' possibilities highlighted above, discussing them in detail with you and working with you to ensure that the finished 'outcomes for pupils' evidence fits the 'outcomes for pupils' criteria. However, if your HMI becomes convinced you are G3, or G4, they'll still be working to get your data to fit their grade – but that won't be a help to you.

---

21. teacherhead.com/2017/02/24/more-issues-with-progress-8/

Those 'lifelines' are very unlikely to be mentioned. Remember, again: the inspection process is subjective. Every decision of your lead inspector and the inspection team is subjective. Best to have your lead inspector approaching your school with a mindset that reflects a glass half-full, than a glass half-empty inspection scenario. It is possible to engineer that scenario through a cogent and persuasive self-evaluation.

THE EFFECTIVENESS OF THE 16-19 STUDY PROGRAMMES

Your sixth form, per se, is not judged on inspection. Instead, the study programmes you offer are inspected. That is a subtle, but important distinction. When a separate grade for post-16 provision was introduced in September 2014, inspectors were still asked to inspect the 'effectiveness of the sixth form provision' with a rider to inspect the 'quality of education provided in the post-16 study programmes'. Ofsted changed this, with the introduction of the common inspection framework in September 2015, to bring 16-19 school inspection more in line with the inspection of further education institutions and to reflect the grade descriptors in the 'further education and skills handbook'. From September 2015 to the present, the 'school handbook' wording relating to sixth for provision is: '**Inspecting the effectiveness of the 16-19 study programmes**'.

If you have a sixth form, the 'effectiveness of your 16-19 study programmes' is given a separate overall grade on inspection, which has separate judgement criteria. A separate section in the handbook is devoted to this (Page 63). All the other major areas of school inspection are inspected during the inspection of the 16-19 study programmes. Inspectors will examine: the effectiveness of leadership and management in the study programmes, the quality of teaching, learning and assessment in the study programmes, the personal development behaviour and welfare of students in the study programmes and the outcomes for learners in the study programmes. There are no numerical grades given, if your inspection is a Section 5 inspection, but instead, grades will be implicit, or even explicit, in the writing.

Thus, in your self-evaluation, write the effectiveness of the 16-19 study programmes as a series of sub-headings for each of the major areas that will be inspected. Apply all the advice contained in the 'self-evaluation' chapters in 'Taking Control'. Sixth form student outcomes data is so specific however and doesn't link easily to Y7-11 data that it should be included here and not in the 'outcomes for pupils' section of your main SEF.

Do remember that you are not writing about your sixth form; you are writing about the 16-19 study programmes you offer in the sixth form.

> *Be prepared and take control via your self-evaluation. Especially around 'outcomes for pupils'. Don't leave your inspection outcome to chance on the day.*

I'll now merge back my two separated strands of primary and secondary SEF guidance into one narrative. From now on, I'll give examples from both phases within the overall narrative. Please skip, if an example doesn't apply to your school.

2.4 SEF Writing: The Effectiveness of Leadership and Management

Ofsted say that 'effectiveness of leadership and management' (L&M for our purposes) is their number one priority on inspection. I disagree and believe me, it is 'outcomes for pupils' that is most likely to determine your overall inspection grade, not L&M. If outcomes are less than 'Good', only the presence of a new SLT, who are working well, have strengths and clear capacity to improve, will save L&M from ending up the same grade.

L&M provides plenty of opportunities for slip-ups, though and if L&M itself is judged as 'Requires improvement', it is very unlikely that 'overall effectiveness' would be judged as 'Good'. Let's avoid the banana skins and understand the grade fully. If L&M is judged as 'Inadequate', your school is likely to go into 'Special Measures'.

Don't be afraid to talk highly of the headteacher/Principal in your SEF. If you are writing the section yourself, it can be a very unnatural thing to do, but remember your audience. Your HMI/OI does not know your school and will only have the previous Ofsted's comments to go by and those may well have been about a different headteacher. The quality of leadership provided by the headteacher is important to the inspection team, so if you are a 'Good' school; write yourself as at least good and that your work has been crucial to the school being that grade. To help you, because I know that writing this can feel uncomfortable, use comments about you from others, perhaps from LA school improvement visits, or Ofsted monitoring visits.

The translation of the headteacher/Principal's vision to all leaders and staff is important and the way this has been formulated with governors and communicated to all staff, constitutes the first grade descriptor in the 'effectiveness of leadership and management'. That's not a random arrangement and is an indicator of its importance to Ofsted and their inspectors. As such, a comment about your vision and how you have communicated that to all staff, would sit better right at the start of your SEF, in your context statement.

Leadership starts with the HT/Principal, but needs to be evidenced at all levels, including in governance. If your governors don't work as an effective team, again, it is unlikely that L&M will be judged as 'Good'.

The bullet point criteria within the grade descriptors (Pages 41 to 43) require particular areas to be written carefully in your SEF. Some are so important, that they require separate sub-headings, as they are 'limiting grades'. Two such 'limiting grades' are defined in the 'Inadequate' criteria for 'overall effectiveness' (Page 36). These are safeguarding and the promotion on pupils' spiritual, moral, social and cultural education. However, the handbook goes much further. In the criteria for 'Inadequate' L&M (Page 43) if any of these things are inadequate, L&M is likely to be inadequate. If L&M are judged 'Inadequate' then overall effectiveness is also likely to be Grade 4. These are above and beyond the other major assessment areas, discussed in other 'SEF writing' chapters and none of these will be given an outright grade. These are:

1. **Governance**
2. **The curriculum**
3. **Safeguarding**
4. **The promotion of equality of opportunity**
5. **Protection of pupils from radicalisation and extremist views**
6. **The promotion of traditional British values**

I'll deal with each of these in this section. The first three deserve sub-sections of their own within L&M. The last three can be covered in your general L&M writing.

1. GOVERNANCE

In 'Talk for Teaching' governors are another group of people that inspection and school support, has enabled me to see at work in many types of school. I describe them as 'brilliant people' for very good reason.

Inspectors should always remember that governors are volunteers, but the days of cosy chats – for that's often what they were – between lead inspectors and chairs of governors are long gone. Governors, academy trustees and academy sponsors (collectively; 'governors' for the purposes of this book) are very much in the inspection firing line and as such need to be well prepared for inspection.

Because they are volunteers, some governors may not be able to attend inspection, as you only get half a day's notice, but most governing bodies have an Ofsted action plan of their own and have determined a 'first team' pool, for this meeting. 2/3/4 are good numbers, depending upon skills and availability. Just one representative (often the chair) can leave him, or her, exposed and should be avoided if possible.

The questions governors will be asked are encapsulated in the bullets (Page 39, Paragraph 148) of the inspection handbook. Whoever you choose for your team needs to be able to answer questions across that range of questions. The second bullet carries much weight:

> 'Inspectors will consider whether governors:...
>
> * provide a balance of challenge and support to leaders, understanding the strengths and areas needing improvement at the school'

It's worth having some examples up your sleeve where you've both offered support and challenged SLT, with demonstrable outcomes. In addition, don't miss the importance attached to judgements around governor work, contained within the grade descriptors for the 'effectiveness of leadership and management' (Pages 41 and 42).

The other area, over which you mustn't allow yourselves to be tripped up, is safeguarding. Give chapter and verse around your training and demonstrate good knowledge, showing where governors have given support and challenge to the school over any safeguarding issues.

A 2016 article written by Sean Harford (@HarfordSean, on Twitter – Sean is very active and helpful on Twitter, please do follow him), Ofsted's National Director for Education, following a meeting with around 130 National Co-ordinators of Governor Services (NCOGS), provides this useful for governors around inspection:

> educationinspection.blog.gov.uk/2015/10/19/school-governors-and-inspection/

2. THE CURRICULUM

There are two mentions of 'curriculum' in the bullets for what inspectors should consider in judging the effectiveness of leadership and management (Page 37):

* 'the design, implementation and evaluation of the curriculum, ensuring breadth and balance and its impact on pupils' outcomes and their personal, development, behaviour and welfare
* how well the school supports the formal curriculum with extra-curricular opportunities for pupils to extend their knowledge and understanding and to improve their skills in a range of artistic, creative and sporting activities'.

Don't miss extra-curricular activities, but also note that your section about curriculum should also mention how the curriculum supports other areas of the school's work, including: spiritual, moral, social and cultural education, the promotion of fundamental British values, e-safety and the protection of pupils from radicalisation and extremism.

Also, comment on the range of subjects offered, any extras you offer above and beyond the statutory (non-academy) National Curriculum. Say whether you believe your curriculum to be sufficiently broad and balanced if you are an academy. Joanna Hall, Ofsted's Deputy Director of Schools offers advice around a 'broad and balanced' curriculum in this presentation from September 2016:

www.insidegovernment.co.uk/uploads/2016/09/joannahall-1.pdf

If you are a secondary school that has had to cut your curriculum offer, take time to explain that your curriculum is still broad and balanced. In addition, secondary schools, be careful with whether you may be entering pupils for what Ofsted may consider to be 'inappropriate qualifications with subject content overlap'. In the March 2017 Ofsted school inspection update, Issue 9, Ofsted[22] said to their inspectors:

'To assess how well a school provides a broad and balanced curriculum, suitable for all pupils, inspectors must review the design of the curriculum and the suitability of pathways and qualifications for pupils at the school. This is critical in determining whether or not schools are entering large cohorts of pupils for inappropriate qualifications and where there is significant overlap in subject content. These entry patterns do not serve pupils well and in some schools they inhibit positive outcomes for pupils and curtail opportunities for their future.'

There is no definition given of exactly what would be deemed inappropriate content, but have your arguments prepared if you feel that you offer some qualifications that might attract inspector attention.

Be aware that curriculum is also expected to support good teaching and learning. In a presentation on September 27th 2017, Joanna Hall, Ofsted's Deputy Director of

22. www.gov.uk/government/uploads/system/uploads/attachment_data/file/595739/School_inspection_newsletter_March_2017.pdf

schools pointed to four key areas from the handbook (Page 43) section on 'teaching, learning and assessment':

- *'scrutiny of pupils' work, with particular attention to pupils' effort and success in completing their work, both in and outside lessons, so that they can progress and enjoy learning across the curriculum;*
- *how well assessment draws on a range of evidence of what pupils know, understand and can do across the curriculum;*
- *the impact of the teaching of literacy on outcomes across the curriculum;*
- *the impact of pupils' mathematical knowledge, understanding and skills on outcomes across the curriculum.'*

The teaching of both literacy and numeracy across the curriculum are two things to note here and how you tackle both should be mentioned in this 'curriculum' section.

Finally, it is worth illustrating, to secondary readers, the importance to inspection teams of seeing that you have few pupils who go on to be NEET (Not in Education, Employment, or Training). I'll use an inspection example. A criterion within the descriptors for personal development, behaviour and welfare (Page 51) is the critical one, but it is the effectiveness of your curriculum that is key and it therefore reflects upon the overall quality of L&M:

- *'the extent to which all pupils attain relevant qualifications so that they can and do progress to the next stage of their education into courses that lead to higher level qualifications or into jobs that meet local and national needs.'*

I led the inspection of a secondary school several years ago, where NEETs were zero and had been for two years. You don't often see that, though I've just been fortunate to support a school with zero NEETs, despite attainment on entry being well into the blue of sig- in every year group. Zero NEETs impressed the team enormously and helped to nudge the school closer to 'Outstanding'. It really is rather brilliant of a school to have no NEETs, especially if the catchment has a degree of difficulty and disadvantage. This is all about life chances and disadvantaged pupils have the chance to continue their catch-up in the next stage of their education (disadvantage which they brought to their early years setting, years ago and follows them all the way through school), continuing to learn in the sixth form, further education institution, or in a job.

If your school does well here and has few NEETs, shout about your success in your SEF!

3. SAFEGUARDING

A school's first duty to parents is to keep their children safe. When a parent leaves their child at the school gates (or when the very large 16-yr-old walks through them!) you are in effect agreeing to allow the teachers and other staff at the school to act 'in loco parentis'. This was enshrined in common law as far back as 1893, when a court held that 'the schoolmaster is bound to take such care of his pupils as a careful father would'. It has been updated since(!) but the principle remains in law. Pupils must be kept safe. Thus, safeguarding is the number one priority on inspection and is also a 'limiting judgement' on inspection. If safeguarding is inadequate in your school, you are likely to go straight into 'Special Measures' (Page 36).

Evidence safeguarding with as much numerical data as you can. Pupil voice evidence is good here, as is data from parent questionnaires. If your school is a veritable sanctuary, for many very deprived and challenged children, your inspectors will see that, but highlight the fact in your SEF.

Safeguarding is so big a part of inspection that it has its own 35-page set of guidance for inspectors.[23] They must know it and so must you as a school.

Ofsted expect also instruct their inspectors to be familiar with two other pieces of statutory guidance in relation to safeguarding and thus, so should you be familiar with them too.[24, 25]

To go through the intricacies of safeguarding is too big a scope for a section of this book, but if you get safeguarding wrong on a daily basis and beyond simple administrative errors, which can easily be corrected on inspection, you are not doing right by the pupils in your school and lead inspectors and inspection teams will not be kind. Nor should they be.

---

23. www.gov.uk/government/publications/inspecting-safeguarding-in-early-years-education-and-skills-from-september-2015

24. 'Keeping children safe in education: Statutory guidance for schools and colleges' www.gov.uk/government/publications/keeping-children-safe-in-education--2

25. 'Working together to safeguard children' www.gov.uk/government/publications/working-together-to-safeguard-children--2

Worth mentioning your website and whether it is compliant here. Your lead inspector has to state whether it is compliant with statutory expectations and also has to state where it is not compliant. To do that, of course, you must ensure that it is! All information that you should put in your website can be found here:

www.gov.uk/guidance/what-maintained-schools-must-publish-online

A couple of recent examples of non-compliant website comments in recent inspection reports are these. The first is from a primary school:

> *'The school does not meet requirements on the publication of information about the allocation and impact of the pupil premium and sports funding, the SEN information report, information about governors, equality objectives and the school's complaints policy on its website. Some of this information does not comply because it is incomplete, or is out of date.'*

The second from a secondary school:

> *'The school does not meet requirements on the publication of information about a named person for enquiries; the school's most recent results at key stage 4 with regard to attainment 8 and English baccalaureate subjects; the behaviour policy does not cover search, restraint or force or powers beyond the gate; the report for special educational needs does not mention evaluation, assessing and reviewing; and governance does not include the structure of sub-committees nor a register of interests on its website.'*

Not too much to worry about here, as both schools remained 'Good', but it's a little embarrassing to have this in your report for years to come and it's not worth the risk of being badly tripped up by a non-compliant website.

It is also worth following the link to 'advice on publishing information about your school's governors', which is contained within the DfE advice as to what to publish online, because buried in this is what you should publish on your website regarding governors' interests. Paragraph 30 of this rather difficult to find, but important, governance document, is here:

www.gov.uk/government/uploads/system/uploads/attachment_data/ file/558622/2012_Constitution_Regulations_Statutory_Guidance__-_Sept_16.pdf

If your website is compliant, say so. In addition, to help your LI, add a sentence like this (or copy, as long as it is true): 'there is no negative information, safeguarding or otherwise, of which we are aware, on the Internet, or in the local press, from the RSC, LA, DfE, or police, concerning our pupils'.

Safeguarding is not graded, but this handbook point says what inspectors must do and why there is always a separate written judgement on safeguarding (Page 17):

> *'inspectors will always make a written judgement under leadership and management in the report about whether or not the arrangements for safeguarding children and learners are effective'.*

4. EQUALITY OF OPPORTUNITY
5. PROTECTION FROM RADICALISATION AND EXTREMISM
6. THE PROMOTION OF TRADITIONAL BRITISH VALUES

There are overlaps between all there, here and overlaps too with curriculum and with SMSC. If you are clever, areas 4, 5 and 6 could be subsumed within SMSC and/or in curriculum in your writing. Inspection expectations are encapsulated in the handbook in these grade descriptors and bullets:

- *'how well leaders and governors promote all forms of equality and foster greater understanding of and respect for people of all faiths (and those of no faith), races, genders, ages, disability and sexual orientations (and other groups with protected characteristics), through their words, actions and influence within the school and more widely in the community'.* (Page 36)
- *'how well the school prepares pupils positively for life in modern Britain and promotes the fundamental British values of democracy, the rule of law, individual liberty and mutual respect for and tolerance of those with different faiths and beliefs and for those without faith'.* (Page 37)
- *'the effectiveness of leaders' and governors' work to raise awareness and keep pupils safe from the dangers of abuse, sexual exploitation, radicalisation and extremism and what the staff do when they suspect that pupils are vulnerable to these issues'.* (Page 37)

Explain how you promote equality of opportunity for all and promote traditional British values through the curriculum/assemblies/tutor groups/specialist curriculum days and especially, perhaps, through your SMSC curriculum. Refer to your 'Prevent duty' training and remind staff of their responsibilities here, as you would all areas of safeguarding. Inspectors will check with them, but again, this is a day-to-day expectation. Also refer to your staff's training in child sexual exploitation (CSE) and female genital mutilation (FGM).

Be especially careful here if you are a faith school. The so-called 'Trojan Horse' affair, where five Birmingham schools were placed in 'Special Measures' in 2014, changed the way Ofsted look at the promotion of traditional British values in all schools. By September 2015, the phrase 'Promotion of traditional British values' (of 'democracy, the rule of law, individual liberty and mutual respect for and tolerance of those with different faiths and beliefs and for those without faith' Page 37) appeared in the inspection handbook. The key word is 'promotion' and there is direct reference to the promotion of traditional British values around tolerance of different faiths and beliefs. A display in the corridor isn't enough and inspectors will delve deeper into curriculum and past records if they feel there is an issue.

It is worth reading the handbook 'Effectiveness of leadership and management' grade descriptors and identifying the references to all these three areas, 4, 5 and 6 and just noting the number of bullets that could render L&M as Grade 4, 'Inadequate' (Pages 41 to 43).

2.5 SEF Writing: Quality of Teaching, Learning and Assessment (TL&A)

With teaching, comes the responsibility to do what is expected of teachers by their school and headteacher. However, those responsibilities must be reasonable and some SLT expectations can cause high workload in the run-up to inspection, if headteachers and senior leaders SLT don't fully understand Ofsted's expectations on them. This grade, 'the quality of teaching learning and assessment', is for leaders to evidence through presentation of their results and their monitoring of the quality of teaching and learning in the school. It is not for teachers to achieve on inspection. As I'll go on to explain, teachers have very little influence upon the grade awarded for TL&A during inspection. Hence this, about which I feel strongly:

> The inclusion of 'teaching' in this grade puts both SLT and teachers under pressure to somehow get it right on the day. That can put unnecessary work on to classroom teachers and their assistants (to whom I'll refer to, collectively, as 'teachers'). Headteachers and SLT have a responsibility to reduce that workload as far as possible and I believe that the inspection workload for teachers can be reduced to next to nothing. Much of this chapter will be an argument that teachers don't have to do anything further than following everyday school policy and speaking positively to inspectors. After reading this chapter, you may wonder why the quality of teaching is graded on inspection at all.

So how should you prepare?

Ofsted don't grade lessons any more and indeed haven't graded lessons since the end of Section 10 inspections in 2005. They did, however, create enormous confusion amongst everyone by still giving a grade for quality of teaching seen during a lesson observation (for which at least a 20 minute visit was needed) for another 9 years. Finally, grades for anything to do with teaching, or learning, following lesson visits, were ended in summer 2014.

Ofsted have produced an excellent set of 'mythbusters' in the inspection handbook, under 'Clarification for schools' (Pages 9 and 10), a major one being:

1. 'Ofsted **does not** award a grade for the quality of teaching or outcomes in the individual lessons visited. It **does not** grade individual lessons. It **does not** expect schools to use the Ofsted evaluation schedule to grade teaching or individual lessons.'

The emboldened words are Ofsted's from the handbook. However, teachers simply don't believe that they are not being, in some way, graded. A simple Twitter poll in March 2017, to which 657 people responded, showed that over 76% of teachers felt that when an Ofsted inspector was in their room, they still felt their teaching was being graded.[26]

The TES said a similar thing on 13th March 2017:

In the article, Geoff Barton, general secretary of the Association of School and College Leaders, said that:

'it was understandable that teachers would be anxious about the presence of an inspector at the back of their classrooms. "Probably the best way of puncturing that is to be very clear about what inspectors are doing there," he said. "Are they looking at students' behaviour? Are they looking at the quality of marking in the books? Teachers would probably be very reassured to know what it is they are looking at.'[27]

This shows that a large body of teachers (and probably a significant number of SLT) still don't believe that lessons aren't somehow graded, three years on from the removal of any grades. I back Ofsted here to a degree. Lessons aren't graded and there is no covert aggregation of secret grades. Really, there isn't! But three years on you'd think this message would have got home. It clearly hasn't. The message and the 'mythbuster' haven't managed to convince anything like all teachers and while ever Ofsted judge the quality of teaching overall in a school, this belief that grading is somehow occurring, covertly, or otherwise, is bound to perpetuate.

I'd come to the conclusion that giving a grade for the quality of teaching seen in a 20-30 minute lesson visit was, quite frankly, silly, long before Ofsted stopped.

---

26. twitter.com/PaulGarvey4/status/844450259287900161
27. www.tes.com/news/school-news/breaking-news/teachers-still-convinced-ofsted-grades-their-lessons

I still had to give a grade, following a lesson visit however. This left my team inspectors and myself, having to feed back, to a gaggle of worried teachers, words (not grades!) which would convey the gist of (but not show outright!) the grade we'd given the quality of teaching in the time we'd been in the room! How utterly confusing for everyone concerned. Then if an inspector slipped and mentioned grades, even obliquely (a heinous crime) I was expected to give the poor soul a ticking off!

I know. It was barmy, but Ofsted kept up this pretence that aggregating – no, wait a minute, we weren't actually supposed to aggregate, but really, we did some kind of aggregation – the grades for quality of teaching seen in all the lessons on a 2-day inspection, somehow gave an accurate impression of the teaching that took place in a school over time. I was so glad when this nonsense finally came to an end in 2014!

What happened, in most inspections, was that the quality of teaching (now the 'quality of teaching learning and assessment') ended up the same grade as 'achievement' (now outcomes for pupils). No wonder when you think about it.

As a result of this, a number of schools were graded as 'Outstanding' but the quality of teaching was only graded 'Good'. This was mainly because not enough 'outstanding lessons' were seen over two days so the 'aggregation' left quality of teaching overall only 'Good'. Potty.

Teachers teach over years, not just two days. This did lead to a recognition by HMCI that schools couldn't really be outstanding, if quality of teaching wasn't outstanding too, so these G1 schools, who had a G2 for quality of teaching, ended up being inspected and were not initially exempt.

Now, if you are 'Outstanding', you are exempt from inspection. Simple as that. And that's potty too. Many others and myself feel that all schools should be inspected on a regular basis, including 'Outstanding' schools, but I've already been through the cost reasons why I feel all G1 schools are unlikely to be inspected, as part of a regular inspection cycle, any time soon.

Currently, the inspection handbook makes it very clear in the criteria for 'overall effectiveness' that for a school to be 'Outstanding', the 'quality of teaching learning and assessment' must be 'Outstanding' too (Page 36). There is no leeway for inspectors any more; the grade for 'overall effectiveness' and for 'quality of teaching and learning' must match for a school to be 'Outstanding'. Similarly, if a school is to be judged as 'Good' for 'overall effectiveness', the 'quality of teaching and learning must also be judged as 'Good' (Page 36). If the quality of 'teaching learning and assessment' has not reached 'Good', the school will not be 'Good' overall. The 'Good' grade descriptor for 'overall effectiveness' (Page 36) clearly states:

'GOOD (2)

- *The quality of teaching, learning and assessment is at least good.'*

The other possible exception to the old 'matching grades rule', of 'achievement' to 'quality of teaching', was if teaching had improved rapidly and recently, but it hadn't yet had long enough to impact upon pupil outcomes. In this case, outcomes – and therefore overall effectiveness – would have been judged a G3, but teaching was judged G2. This is still technically possible, but how exactly are inspectors supposed to judge this, over just two days, when teachers could have worked themselves silly to prepare 'Ofsted' lessons and pupils could have been coached to behave well in class? The judgement is so subjective.

In the past, inspectors were expected to take into account three years of past data. Even if there had been a real turnaround in the last 12-18 months, at that time, the school could still have been graded 'satisfactory' overall on its past achievement. However, both 'quality of teaching' and 'leadership and management could have been a G2'. Again, technically, this is still possible, but it occurs rarely.

This could be examined in the reverse way. If a school is 'Good' overall, then the 'quality of teaching, learning and assessment' must have been good enough to get it to that standard. That sounds eminently sensible.

Lesson visits are important for other things, apart from all the things in the handbook around quality of teaching. They give an excellent opportunity to work with leaders and to assess their skills. Not just around lesson observation; you are constantly picking up the quality of the knowledge that leaders have around pedagogy and leadership skills. You also see the way that the leaders work with staff. I organised learning walks with leaders to start each of my inspections and if I had team members, I would link them to work with a member of senior leadership until break, with the instruction to get into at least one lesson every 10-15 minutes. I'd usually take the headteacher with me, because a lead inspector is tasked with making a good relationship and this gave me a good chance to see the head, or Principal's, way of thinking early in the inspection.

In these learning walks, I'd instruct my team to:

- look at books, to see if marking followed school policy and whether pupils took pride in their work;
- to look at pupils' behaviour and see if the school's behaviour policy was being applied;
- to look at assessment methods and how teachers used them in line with school policy;
- to speak with the teacher and support staff, (when possible);
- to speak with pupils.

Other lead inspectors, Ofsted Inspectors, or Her Majesty's Inspectors, will organise their inspections in their way, but be prepared for any of these things to happen. Especially be prepared for your inspector looking at many more things than the 'quality of teaching, learning and assessment' on a lesson visit. Also, be prepared for an inspector to still sit, observe and take notes – this can still happen! Within guidelines, each lead inspector has their own way of leading and each team inspector has their own way of operating.

In previous frameworks, the link between quality of teaching (as it was) and achievement was very clear. For instance in the 2014 (September) handbook, which has now been withdrawn, the first grade descriptor for 'Outstanding' read:

> 'Much teaching over time in all key stages and most subjects is outstanding and never less than consistently good. As a result, almost all pupils currently on roll in the school, including disabled pupils, those who have special educational needs, disadvantaged pupils and the most able, are making sustained progress that leads to outstanding achievement.'

'Outstanding' teaching (OK, 'Never less than consistently good teaching' was the exact wording – whatever exactly that meant!) would lead to most pupils making rapid and sustained progress. Inspectors had leeway to judge within this subjective criterion exactly what was meant by 'rapid and sustained progress' and what exactly what was meant by 'never less than consistently good teaching'. The current 2016 handbook says nothing of the sort and every criterion is around what teachers do, how pupils learn and a single criterion around information given to parents around assessment. (Pages 47 and 48)

That sounds laudable, but how do you judge that on inspection? These pedagogical criteria cannot be aggregated, so how do you judge if and to what extent, all teachers in the school are doing these things and to what extent pupils are learning as a result, in a day, or two days? Problems surround the judgement for the 'quality of teaching, learning and assessment', which must be judged overall for the school, but must never be specific to any lessons that inspectors visit.

In addition, it is quite possible for teachers, collectively, to get superb results without focussing on many of the handbook criteria. Should inspectors therefore downgrade TL&A for not fulfilling enough of the Ofsted criteria for either 'Good' or 'Outstanding'? You must then downgrade the school overall. These are the questions with which inspection teams wrestle and it does make inspection an intellectually stimulating activity. Unfortunately these are also questions that lead to teachers having doubts about the inspection process, as lesson observations are **the** key area for classroom teachers and their support staff, (i.e. most people in schools) during inspection.

On inspection, what counts, if you are a classroom teacher, or teaching assistant are the visits by inspectors to your lessons. That causes the pressure and the worry. However, if teaching is not in any way being judged, this can give schools a chance to remove classroom teachers from inspection preparation. This could lift a great deal of pressure from your teachers.

Despite what teachers and some SLT still think, teaching is definitely not graded, even covertly, during lesson observations. Your quality of teaching is **not** being judged on a lesson visit and your school's 'quality of teaching, learning and assessment grade' will in almost all aspects, be determined by your school's other outcomes and certainly not by you!

I don't feel that teaching should be graded at all on inspection and to be fair, Nicky Morgan's white paper of March 2016 'Educational Excellence Everywhere' shows that the DfE and Ofsted are thinking along the same lines:[28]

> 7.21 'Despite recent reforms and clarifications, such as Ofsted no longer judging the quality of individual lessons and confirming they do not have a preferred teaching style, some schools continue to tell us that they feel they are judged on whether or not they follow particular styles of teaching,'

and:

> 7.23 'Under the proposals, inspectors would continue to report on the "impact" of teaching through the other three judgements, but they would no longer publish a separate grade for schools based on the quality of teaching.

Sandwiched between these two is 7.22:

> 'High quality teaching is, of course, vital. Teaching, learning and assessment are a school's core business. However, as set out in chapter 2, we believe that **it is for schools and teachers to decide how to teach** – and that schools should be held to account primarily for the outcomes their pupils achieve'.

And this led Nicky Morgan, in the same white paper, to state:

> 'Ofsted will consult on removing the separate graded judgments on the quality of teaching, learning and assessment to help clarify that the focus of inspection is on outcomes and to reduce burdens on schools and teachers.'

Ofsted haven't yet carried out that consultation and they have no plans to radically alter the inspection framework in summer 2017. As they have also promised not to greatly change the handbook mid-year, the results of any consultation will not produce changes in the handbook regarding the removal of this teaching grade until

---

28. www.gov.uk/government/uploads/system/uploads/attachment_data/file/508447/ Educational_Excellence_Everywhere.pdf

summer 2018 at the earliest. In my view, that is a pity and will lead to a continuing fear, amongst teachers and SLT, of some kind of inspector grading. This, in turn, will lead many schools and teachers to still try to produce 'Ofsted lessons' with only half-a-day's notice, to try to impress inspectors and it will continue to produce an unnecessary spike in workload and stress. There is absolutely no need to do this, no matter what kind of school you are, or what kind of grade you may be.

Over a year has now passed since the publication of this white paper. We have a new education secretary and precisely *nothing* has happened to change this unfortunate situation where teachers are still being put under pressure by an Ofsted visit because of worries that they and their school will be held accountable for the teaching seen, in lessons, over the course of their inspection.

Something here is wrong.

SO WHY JUDGE QUALITY OF TEACHING (LEARNING AND ASSESSMENT) AT ALL?
Ofsted's current position on looking at the quality of teaching, learning and assessment, as explained by their National Director, Education, in their 'School Inspection Update', March 2017, Issue: 9 is this:

> *'Finally, I know that schools have been appreciative of our move over two years ago to stop grading the quality of teaching in individual lessons. The evidence supporting the overall judgement for quality of teaching, learning and assessment has not been diminished by this move and it has helped support those schools that wished to stop grading individual lessons themselves. However, when observing lessons and feeding back to teachers afterwards, we must not give the incorrect impression that any graded judgement has been formed. In line with our training, we should only use our observations during individual lessons to establish strengths and areas for improvement that, in discussion with others on the inspection team, help to identify and synthesise the common strengths and areas for improvement across the school. In this way, the judgement of the overall quality of teaching, learning and assessment is agreed.'*[29]

---

29. www.gov.uk/government/uploads/system/uploads/attachment_data/file/595739/School_inspection_newsletter_March_2017.pdf

Convinced? Confused? I think it's a dog's breakfast of a grade, still badly misunderstood by teachers and SLT alike, despite Ofsted's best efforts at 'mythbusting'. It is time the 'quality of teaching, learning and assessment' was subsumed into other sections and judged via the outcomes of those.

WHAT SHOULD YOU DO TO PREPARE FOR YOUR INSPECTION OF 'QUALITY OF TEACHING LEARNING AND ASSESSMENT' IN YOUR SCHOOL?
So what should you do as a school in observing your teachers at times other than inspection? Should you carry on grading, so teachers learn to produce 'tick-list' lessons where they can demonstrate all the different elements of pedagogy contained in the criteria for 'Good', or 'Outstanding', teaching, as seen in the handbook (Pages 47 and 48)? I'm very clear that this is a **'No! No! Definitely not!'** That would take us back to square one and put horrible pressure on teachers to conform to the pedagogy contained therein. That would be all wrong. If a teacher gets good results and is doing nothing illegal, or unethical, they should be allowed to teach however the hell they want!

I'd strongly advise a 'carry on as usual' approach to teaching during an inspection. That may appear to run counter to my opening inspection mantra of 'praemonitus, praemunitus', but in this case, you are already forearmed and forewarned. Whatever quality of teaching you have in your school has already been demonstrated by the progress of your pupils to date, especially those currently on roll. They have already learned, to the day of the inspection. They have already been assessed. The books have already been marked as per school policy (hopefully). Beyond following school behaviour policy in lessons on the day, and speaking positively (hopefully) with your inspectors, nothing that happens in lessons during the course of your inspection will, or at least, should, change the overall grade for 'teaching learning and assessment' that you will be awarded.

This next paragraph is one for the teachers:

As a result, beyond the caveats below, I would advise you to tell your staff to do **nothing** extra. Don't do any extra preparation. Don't mark extra. Don't teach any differently. Just come in and do your job, as you would if inspectors weren't there. **Nothing** you can do extra on those days, or specifically for those days, will change your grade for the 'quality of teaching learning and assessment'. **Nothing**. Just greet the inspector and senior leader if they come into your room and chat to them positively about the school and what your pupils are doing. Inspection, for teachers and their assistants, really can be as relaxed as that, as long as these two caveats are fulfilled:

1. Marking

Ofsted have these, very sensible, 'mythbusters' (Pages 9 and 10):

> 'Ofsted **does not** expect to see a particular frequency or quantity of work in pupils' books or folders. Ofsted recognises that the amount of work in books and folders will depend on the subject being studied and the age and ability of the pupils'.

And:

> 'Ofsted recognises that marking and feedback to pupils, both written and oral, are important aspects of assessment. However, Ofsted **does not** expect to see any specific frequency, type or volume of marking and feedback; these are for the school to decide through its assessment policy. **Marking and feedback should be consistent with that policy**, which may cater for different subjects and different age groups of pupils in different ways, in order to be effective and efficient in promoting learning.'
> (My stars to highlight).

The key for SLT and teachers on inspection is that marking and assessment should follow school policy; nothing more. If a teacher isn't doing this and it is picked up on inspection, this is likely to be addressed through the 'effectiveness of leadership and management' as this issue is likely to have been longstanding and **could** be having a detrimental effect on pupil progress. Teachers in a school have this responsibility and must have their books marked and assessed in line with school policy. The school policy will vary from school to school and Ofsted, rightly, in my opinion, feel this is fine.

The other thing that inspectors will look for in pupils' books is around the first criterion bullet in the 'Good' descriptors for 'personal development, behaviour and welfare' (Page 52). Inspectors will look to see whether pupils; 'take pride in their work'. The outstanding criterion (Page 51), as is the case with many G1/G2 criteria throughout the handbook, does not have a direct mirror to this.

2. Behaviour

If poor behaviour happens in a lesson, or around school, just follow the school's behaviour policy. Show inspectors that you understand what to do, deal with the incident, take a deep breath and carry on, as you would in a normal day.

These two caveats are just part and parcel of the day job. Teachers have responsibilities on every working day. This day should not be different to any other.

For teachers, my advice is to 'take charge' too. The inspector will step into yours and your pupils' territory. Your classroom is your daily workplace and is not suddenly owned by an Ofsted inspector for 20 minutes. Don't be in any way cowed. Smile. Greet your inspector when they visit. Direct them to any documentation you may have. Allow your pupils to feel your confidence. When you get a chance, go over and engage the inspector in conversation – this can be a great idea for showing off your success stories in terms of pupil progress, especially the progress of Pupil Premium pupils or disadvantaged pupils (disadvantage can be wider than just PP, or SEND pupils, though ASP contains an Ofsted definition). 'Did you know that Sam has made terrific progress...' This can send such positive messages to inspectors. SLT and HTs; support your teachers in this! Let them just be themselves on inspection with no extra expectations about teaching performance.

Notwithstanding these two caveats, there is no reason why inspection should not be a normal working day for teachers. Gone are the days when, with an inspection in a G2/G3 balance after a poor first day of teaching seen, a headteacher could say to his lead inspector (this actually happened in 2013, in a large school I supported); 'I'll give you 15 people to see tomorrow and all will teach 'Good' lessons to show how good this school really is'. They all did teach 'Good' lessons, after a superhuman evening of preparation and this performance impressed inspectors to the degree that the school ended up Grade 2. 'Quality of teaching' (as it was then) was judged Grade 2 and thus the school could be judged G2 for overall effectiveness, as the arguments we constructed in the SEF were recognised by the team. A couple of years later, the headteacher said the G2 judgement given in that inspection was worth over half a million pounds to that school, in terms of extra pupil recruitment alone. The high stakes outcomes of inspection grades.

Today, the teaching is seen on inspection won't be graded anyway and there may not be a second day. It will make so little difference to your inspection, beyond giving your lead inspector examples of good, or poor, practice to put in the report and confirming the school's view of the 'quality of teaching learning and assessment'. If the inspection outcome is G2, the lead inspector will choose the good examples to put in the report. If the inspection is G3, the lead inspector will choose poorer examples, with reference to better examples, only to show that an overall teaching weakness has the potential to be addressed if practice is better shared. As I've said; the process is subjective and report writing can and will be moulded to fit the evidence contained in the evidence base.

I feel that there's a very strong argument for dropping the grade for teaching, learning and assessment from inspectors' work on inspection and judging this by outcomes and not by observation. It is effectively redundant, as far as the inspection goes, because next to nothing inspectors will see on those inspection days will change their minds about this grade. If it does change the grade, it shouldn't: all inspectors see of the school is a snapshot of a school's work. Only inertia is now keeping the grade there. Ofsted's laudable statement that no major revisions of the framework will take place mid-year and also in 2017 are having an unfortunate corollary that is extending that inertia. They are in a cleft stick. The government's white paper recognised that the situation needs to change – and I suspect Ofsted recognise that it needs to change too – but Ofsted won't change the framework any time soon. Having said that, I doubt that quality of TL&A will be a separate grade in 2020.

Teaching is always a privilege to see, but it is not possible to give advice as to how all teachers in the school should improve their teaching after a limited number of lesson visits in an inspection. This is especially true in secondary schools, where not all teachers will be seen and possibly not even all subjects. Visits to a teacher's lessons are often short and usually not repeated, so no inspector is capable of giving pithy advice about long-term improvement, even to a single teacher on the basis of such short visits. That's for the school to do. SLT see teachers' work over a long period of time. Good luck to inspectors who have to feed back to staff. I do hope your music experience is deep enough to advise a music teacher on exactly how he/she should improve their subject teaching after a single, one-off, 20-minute observation.

So, as a school, please save your teachers a great deal of work and anxiety and leave teaching alone, when preparing for inspection. Trust that it will look after itself.

The school leadership have quite enough other things to do that really can influence inspectors. Instead of worrying about teaching, concentrate on the other areas of your preparation where you really can make a crucial difference to your grades.

On inspection, don't worry unduly about your grade for the quality of 'teaching, learning and assessment'. Much has already been written in the stone of your other outcomes.

2.6 SEF Writing: Personal Development, Behaviour and Welfare (PDB&W)

Use your SEF to give pointers to your inspectors as to where they will see good (or better) PDB&W around school, but be careful not to just give provision and description of what behaviour, especially, is like. Always link provision to outcomes (explain the impact of what you have done). Link PDB&W to teaching, learning and assessment outcomes and to the impact of leaders' vision, intervention and initiatives. Use numerical data wherever you can.

There is specific data you can include, like attendance and exclusions data and data from other school logs, but also use pupil and parent surveys here and comments from other sources that speak favourably about the PDB&W of your pupils and corroborate your views.

Be aware that 'personal development and welfare' will get its own section in your report, as will 'behaviour' (Inspectors have to write a 'clear, written judgment' about both (Page 50, Paragraph 165). Be prepared for that by dividing this judgment area into those two, separate, sections in your SEF. The overall judgment given will be the lowest common denominator. If 'behaviour' is judged a Grade 3, but 'personal development and welfare' is judged Grade 2, the overall grade for 'personal development, behaviour and welfare' will be judged as 'Requires improvement'. Similarly, if 'behaviour' is judged a Grade 1, but 'personal development and welfare' is judged Grade 2, the overall grade for 'personal development, behaviour and welfare' will be judged as 'Good'.

This gives inspectors more room to judge PDB&W as a lower grade, as each of the two effectively limits the grade. A major Ofsted complaint about its inspectors was that the old 'Behaviour and Safety' grade, (which you may have received on your last inspection, if it was pre-July 2015) was too often a grade higher than other grades. Most especially, in 'Good' schools, behaviour was judged as 'Outstanding'. It is still possible for PDB&W to be Grade 3, but 'overall effectiveness' be a Grade 2, but is less likely to happen than it was before the last major revision of the handbook in August 2015 and can, ostensibly, only happen now in 'exceptional circumstances' (Page 36):

'All other key judgements are likely to be good or outstanding. In exceptional circumstances, one of the key judgement areas may require improvement, as long as there is convincing evidence that the school is improving it rapidly and securely towards good.'

'Ostensibly' though! Yet again, the criterion gives inspectors leeway in their judgement and thus scope for you to persuade. If you know that everything else in your school is good but behaviour is in some way not, perhaps due to legacy issues of previous leadership not tackling it effectively enough, show that it is improving rapidly under new leadership. This could mean that 'overall effectiveness' still remains a Grade 2, if your short inspection converts, or your Section 5 inspection team decide on Grade 2 and not Grade 3 (or Grade 3 and not Grade 4) for 'personal development behaviour and welfare'.

Looking at the grade descriptors for 'Outstanding' PDB&W, there is a criterion on which I have already commented, in talking about the curriculum in 'the effectiveness of leadership and management' (**section 2.4**).

'Pupils understand how their education equips them with the behaviours and attitudes necessary for success in their next stage of education, training or employment and for their adult life.'

'Preparation for the next stage of education' is a phrase that crops up several times around careers in the inspection handbook, but getting pupils 'next-stage ready' is wider than that and encompasses aspirations, behaviours and attitudes. You could link what you do to promote good pupil success in the next stage of their education in terms of behaviours and attitudes to your writing about the curriculum. No NEETs can be a persuasive factor.

Safeguarding overlaps into 'personal development and welfare', though this is tackled earlier in the book (**Section 2.4** again). That's where you should write about safeguarding in your SEF. Pupils 'being safe and feeling safe at all times' (Page 51, 10th Bullet), is an outcome of good safeguarding practice. As I've said; a school's first duty to parents is to keep their children safe. You should already have evidenced how safe you keep pupils so a reference to that is all that is required here.

SMSC (Spiritual, Moral, Social and Cultural education) also overlaps into PDB&W, in terms of pupils being 'thoughtful caring and active citizens in school and in the wider society). (Page 52, Top Bullet) Evidence this in the 'effectiveness of leadership and management' (**section 2.4**) of your SEF.

Attendance and punctuality (Page 50, Paragraph 167). Attendance can be a limiting judgement. Punctuality is unlikely to be so. By a 'limiting judgement', Ofsted mean that, if attendance is poor and not improving, it can limit your overall effectiveness grade to Grade 4; 'Inadequate'. That seems scary, but I've never seen a school hanged simply on attendance. Neither did I hang a school, or was on a team that hanged a school, on attendance either. If a school is clearly 'Good' overall in every other respect, but attendance has been a historical bugbear, I've found ways round it, sometimes with my QA reader's (the person who does quality assurance on your report at Ofsted, or Tribal, as it used to be in the SW) support, to write attendance to fit the 'Good' descriptor somehow.

The attendance limiting statement for PD&WB 'Inadequate' is this (Page 53):

'Attendance is consistently low for all pupils or groups of pupils and shows little sign of sustained improvement.'

This would feed through to a likely 'Inadequate' judgement for overall effectiveness (Page 36).

The judgement on the overall effectiveness is likely to be inadequate where any one of the key judgements is inadequate and/or safeguarding is ineffective and/or there are serious weaknesses in the overall promotion of pupils' spiritual, moral, social and cultural development.'

It just takes just one major judgement to be 'Inadequate' for the school to be 'likely' to be placed in 'Special Measures'. That's why HMI/OI are careful around inspection. If the school is nowhere near Special Measures in all other areas, why condemn it just on attendance? The link between attendance and poor pupil outcomes is not absolute.

If attendance is truly poor, it may well be linked to other 'Inadequate' factors in a failing school and a defence against this limiting judgement would be a waste of time in this circumstance. Accept the Grade 4 for overall effectiveness and move on. *'Taking Control'* can't save you if this is the case.

It's when attendance has been stubbornly low, but pupil progress has remained good, or is accelerating, that attendance can come into play in the judgement for a good school. Lower attendance and poorer pupil progress are certainly related, but by no means always so. I remember well the Local Authority where I worked getting its best GCSE results for years, in the year that it finished bottom of the attendance tables in the south-west.

The descriptor for Grade 2 that applies to attendance is this (Page 52):

> *'Pupils value their education. Few are absent or persistently absent. No groups of pupils are disadvantaged by low attendance. The attendance of pupils who have previously had exceptionally high rates of absence is showing marked and sustained improvement.'*

The principal factors here are to break attendance down into groups of pupils and analyse attendance patterns, these included, over time. If attendance is low for a particular group, get down to pupil level and explain how a (perhaps very) small number of pupils have skewed your attendance data to make it look low, whereas for all other pupils in that group, attendance has been improving (if, of course, that is true). Also, look at overall attendance over time and compare past information from RAISE/ASP to the attendance to date in the current inspection year, if this shows any improvement, it may be enough to help your lead inspector and keep you away from G4.

To convince for G2 is harder if you have lower attendance, but two factors may work in your favour.

Firstly there are no limiting judgments in the Grade 2 descriptors for 'personal development, behaviour and welfare', including the criterion about attendance. The overall judgement has to be a 'best fit'. This requirement also prefaces the grade descriptors for all other judgement areas, apart from 'overall effectiveness' and is an important point to note. If almost all other judgements are satisfied, remind your lead inspector of this. If they won't listen and are singling out attendance, unfairly, as a reason why PDB&W is not Grade 2; complain immediately. This may not go anywhere, as the team may feel that attendance is the anchor to further improvement and must therefore receive a higher weighting in the team's deliberations around the grade, but it's well worth a try, as their evidence for that attendance anchor has to be sound.

Secondly, what exactly is meant by; 'Few are absent or persistently absent'? If you disaggregate your weakest attenders, for the good reasons you present (in the spread sheet of your outliers, perhaps), most pupils may be attending well, or at least better, than RAISE/ASP suggests. Also, a calculation of the average number of days per week, this better attending and larger, group of pupils miss, can make your attendance look better(!).

If you are looking like a G2 school to your lead HMI/OI, they will work with you to prevent attendance limiting your judgement. If you are looking like a G3/4 school, your poor attendance figures may be used as a factor in evidencing that grade. Again, this is subjective and although Inspection dashboard can highlight 'poor' attendance, quite starkly, as a separate statement ('in the lowest 10%'), attendance is usually not something your lead inspector will want to hang you on, if most other factors point to a good school.

Inspectors will make their judgement about 'personal development, behaviour and welfare' using evidence seen on the inspection as well as evidence of trends over time' (Page 50). Ofsted talks about 'typicality' of behaviour. Use incident logs, exclusion data, discussions with pupils around school and in class to evidence this.

2.7 SEF Writing: Spiritual, moral, social and cultural education (SMSC)

This is a limiting judgement for 'overall effectiveness' and handbook information for the inspection of SMSC sits within 'overall effectiveness' (Pages 35 and 36). It is the only area of inspection that does so. As such, it should sit separately in your SEF.

What is expected of you is clearly set out on these two handbook pages, so use sub-headings and write this to the bullet points on those pages. There is a great deal of overlap with the promotion of equality of opportunity, the protection of pupils from radicalisation and extremism and the promotion of traditional British values, all of which fall within the 'effectiveness of leadership and management' (**Section 2.4**) in the handbook and there's nothing wrong with covering all those here. It would save duplication. In addition, link social and moral education to behaviour and safety outcomes wherever you can.

SECTION 3:
AN INSPECTOR'S
INSPECTION – DURING
AND AFTER
YOUR INSPECTION

I'm poacher-turned-gamekeeper now, helping schools to keep at bay the metaphorical Ofsted foxes and hawks and I thought it would be good for your preparation if I detailed a 'typical' inspection from your inspector's – and especially your lead inspector's – point of view. You won't have seen this before. I'd have thought Ofsted might have produced this kind of document, alongside their 'mythbusters', as it could help to demystify the HMI/OI's role and maybe one day, they will.

In this section, I'll cover what will happen during and after inspection, but through an inspector's eyes. It will give you a different perspective and hopefully a different learning experience to continue to uncover those 'unknown unknowns' in the inspection process.

I'll write much of this section through the eyes of your next lead inspector via my own experience and I'm writing this specifically to the headteacher or Principal, though I hope it will be interesting to others to read too. I'll allude to HMI work in a short, Section 8 inspection and I'll reference what they have to do, but I've never been a HMI. HMI, or Ofsted inspectors who lead such short inspections, would not be allowed by Ofsted to give their personal interpretations of this process in public. They would have to leave Ofsted to do it.

As an aside, being a HMI would actually have driven me spare! I wrote in 'Talk for Teaching' that I don't do bosses well – hence my building up and running my company, QA South-West. Working under the crazily strict guidelines of Ofsted would never have been a bag I could have carried very far.

Good luck to HMI though. You have my great respect. HMI are almost all experienced, personable and often consummate professionals who work well with schools and inspect with great knowledge. Their work in supporting G4 and G3 schools to improve, especially prior to the appearance of Regional Schools Commissioners, who have completely disrupted the process via forced Academisation, was very good and was often praised by schools. HMI really do care about school improvement. It's just a pity there aren't enough of them to properly support all the G4/G3 schools to get to 'Good'. It's also a pity that such excellent work will effectively stop, as now there is little need. RSC's are likely to ensure that MATs will take over the work of supporting, or brokering support for, 'failing' schools.

A digression. I do hate that term 'failing schools' with a vengeance. Many of these schools are failing by a metric that means they are more likely to fail, which is desperately unfair. If a school has a greater proportion of disadvantaged pupils, because it finds itself in a more disadvantaged catchment, it is more likely to have progress scores that are below expected. It's as simple as that. Tom Sherrington (@ teacherhead) shows this very well in secondary his blog, with an analysis of >3000 schools, He plots 'Progress 8' scores against the percentage of 'ever 6 FSM' in each school and the outcome is startling:[30]

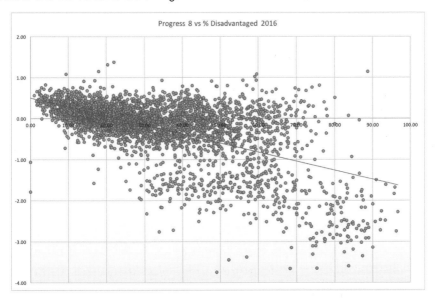

Just look at the numbers of schools with a high number of disadvantaged pupils who had Progress 8 scores below 0.00 (the national average) compared to the number of schools with low numbers of disadvantaged pupils, who had Progress 8 scores below the 0.00 line. This is iniquitous. It's deplorable. It's unfair. It's simply not a level playing field and it is a playing field that has got much more uneven since the demise of CVA (Contextual Value Added) in 2011. Time a measure of CVA was brought back to give today's disadvantaged schools – and their pupils – a better chance on inspection. No pupil can feel good about being in a 'failing school', which is 'failing'

30. teacherhead.com/2017/02/24/more-issues-with-progress-8/

because many disadvantaged pupils, just like them, are in it!. There are calls from many quarters for the return of a CVA measure, rather than the pure 'Value Added' (VA) measure we have now at both Primary and at Secondary. One of those voices is the Headteacher's Roundtable' (on Twitter, a 'think tank' of primary and secondary headteachers, who proposed a 'Multi Year Contextualised Value Added measure' in their 'Alternative Green Paper' of 2016[31]).

Back to an inspector's inspection...

---

31. headteachersroundtable.files.wordpress.com/2016/09/htrt-the-alternative-green-paper-schools-that-enable-all-to-thrive-and-flourish.pdf

3.1 Before the Inspection

Ofsted's factual information, as to what inspector's must do, prior to an inspection, is contained in the handbook (Pages 11 to 19). I'll look at this from the point of view of the person that's about to inspecting you.

I'll begin preparation for inspection as soon as I have notification on the Ofsted inspector's portal that I've been scheduled. This usually happens about 4 weeks before the inspection happens, so yes; I do know your school is coming up for inspection some time before I inspect you. I firstly get an area postcode for the school, then, a little later, your school name. I'll check out your school as soon as I can, sometimes from the area postcode and then I'll do an Internet search for you, have a glance at your website and look up your previous inspection report. Your previous two RAISE reports, or your ASP, in the future, will arrive on the Ofsted inspector's portal shortly after, and I'll look as soon as they arrive. I do all this because I'm interested; every inspector is. This is not just an inspection to be done; this is a school, with real staff and real pupils. I want to get an early sense of the school, before Ofsted send me their information.

Several days before the inspection was scheduled I'll begin work in earnest. Good preparation takes time; for me, a good couple of days. Information has to be analysed and condensed onto to evidence forms (EFs). Before I arrive at your school, I would have separate EFs prepared on:

- your website and whether it was compliant;
- your previous two RAISE/ASP reports;
- your previous L3VA report if you had a sixth form;
- your data dashboard;
- your 'Parent View' (updated during inspection, as there are usually few parental contributions before);
- your Ofsted safeguarding information, to which I would have access via the portal, especially information relating to any qualifying complaints – a 'qualifying complaint' is a complaint upon which Ofsted have decided to act;
- the results of my Internet search for any safeguarding problems, or other major incidents, that made the local press;
- any phone calls to Ofsted that I make to clarify pre-inspection points;
- any other information that I felt needed to be noted (or EFed – a great Ofsted verb!).

I'm constantly thinking of my evidence base both in preparation and during inspection and ensuring it will be compliant with the Ofsted evidence base checklist. Prior to inspection, I would have my EFs 'topped and tailed (numbering all EFs and adding dates and my Ofsted inspection number). I'd also pre-prepare EFs of meetings I knew I would have on inspection, adding a meeting focus.

The fairly laughable thing about all this is that almost all the evidence forms completed on an inspection are **hand-written**! During the course of an inspection, I could easily hand-write 50+ separate EFs, some stretching to several sides. My team would each write 20-30 more. I hand-write shopping lists and Christmas cards, for goodness sake! Ofsted was the only time I actually hand-wrote anything longer than a few words. In addition, each EF has a yellow **carbon copy**(!) that you detach and keep for 6 months, or more if there are any problems with the inspection. How often do you see carbon copies being used today? This writing of evidence forms by hand is like stepping back into the previous century and it really is an area where Ofsted need to drag themselves into the present.

I would also have prepared the basics of my joining instructions to my team, which would contain my evidence trails about which I wanted the team to pay special attention. There would be questions that had arisen from these detailed analyses that I felt need answering. I'll complete these joining instructions following my initial phone call to the headteacher, or Principal and especially after I've read your SEF.

Remember; I have not yet seen anything provided to me by the school, apart from what sits on the school website, so my initial inspection trails have to be based on this. In addition, to my joining instructions, I'll be thinking about my inspection plan and how I'll deploy both my team and myself.

My initial phone call to the headteacher

This all takes time, but the tension really builds with the phone-call to the headteacher. I'm now under time pressure, as I have only that afternoon and evening to complete my final preparation – and I have to appear to be bang on with that preparation and organisation and very much in charge, for the sake of the school and my team. If I am not; the inspection will not go smoothly, as I'll be chasing my tail throughout. The analogy of the duck swimming serenely across a pond, but under the surface the legs are going nineteen to the dozen to power it along, sums up a lead inspector's role during inspection, perfectly.

This is high pressure, high stakes, 'no-mistakes-please', work and provides an answer my opening lines in '*Taking Control*'. You can use this knowledge, that your lead inspector is under time pressure, to good advantage in this lead-up to your inspection, even though you will probably feel like another duck on the same pond!

As a result, I am waiting at home early in the afternoon of the inspection. I used to do the initial phone call, but now Ofsted call. This takes a few administrative things out of my work, but reduces my time for preparation. The call from Ofsted to the school will hopefully be made soon after 12.00. (That's me hoping!) Once I've been notified, I will call you. I'm a little nervous, but I won't show those nerves to you during the call.

I have quite a long list of things to get through in that phone call and information I need to collect. The list can be found in the handbook (Pages 13 to 17), along with a list of school information I can ask for. It is worth noting the depth of information needed, however the Handbook says that the call:

'will be short and focussed on practical issues'.

The call usually takes around 30 minutes and I have a script that I should follow. However, as a headteacher, you've just received a phone call from a stranger – OK, you'll probably know it is Ofsted and you have the right to verify this by halting the conversation and calling the Ofsted helpline for confirmation, should you wish – but you are the one in charge. Your lead inspector is calling you on your territory, not vice-versa. Take a deep breath when the office channels a call from Ofsted to you (I won't have announced to the office that you have an inspection, but on how many days do you get a call from Ofsted?), but remember the 'you are in charge' bit. It can pay dividends if you can use this knowledge to subtly bend the conversation to your angles, knowing that the person you are talking to will soon be under time pressure, if not under time pressure already.

The list of information in the handbook caps what I can ask for and Ofsted don't have any requirement for schools to produce a SEF (Page 17), but I'll bet you are asked whether you have one. At this point, say you do, that it's a working document, so is up-to-date and you will send it soon after this call. This will be very helpful to the person on the other end of the line.

Now be clever and begin to put your SEF preparation to good use...

Ofsted wish this call to be focussed on practical issues; informing parents, documentation, procedure, where to park, will there be any tea and coffee, but you are in charge. Take control when the subject of a SEF comes up and if your lead inspector doesn't introduce it; make sure that you do. Don't just offer the SEF, but commend the 'working document' to your lead inspector. Broach the main positives. Some HMI/OI will stop you there and repeat the Ofsted line – *'just practical issues in this phone call, please'*, but this is your school and most lead inspectors will want to find out as much about it as possible, before contacting their team. If the phone call is 10 minutes longer than planned, that's not going to make much difference to either of you. You can get across the main points of what you are going to show inspectors over the course of the inspection. You can also channel your inspector's way, a measure of your confidence that you really are a 'Good' school, or that you have made significant progress enough to be considered 'Outstanding'. Your inspector may be grateful for extra information that informs the joining instructions and inspection trails. This is a possible opportunity for you to sell your school's position. No need to be pushy, just confident. Radiate a sense that you have been waiting for Ofsted to come in, you are glad of the phone call today and you are confident to talk data and information immediately, if the lead inspector/HMI wishes, because it is something of which you are in full control. All grist to the persuasion mill!

Your HMI/OI will be making notes as the phone call progresses, as another pre-inspection EF has to be completed. It would be good if your lead inspector writes, say; *'HT is confident that the school is now outstanding'* and *'good introductory call'* on this EF. I often used to, as it was evidence to Ofsted that good relationships were being established – establishing good relationships is something that I am tasked to do on inspection.

Immediately after the phone call, a clock is ticking for me. I have to prepare my joining instructions for my team. These are easier to prepare, if I've read your SEF, so I can link to this and give my team a sense of your own judgements and my feelings about them. Make my job in writing my joining instructions as easy as you can for me. Get that persuasive SEF to me quickly, on the back of a good phone call. Drop in your most up to date data and off it goes by 2.00pm. Your IO/HMI will be impressed and rather grateful – not a bad emotional place to have them at this stage.

I also have to prepare an inspection timetable. If I can send this to my team fairly quickly, that is a bonus. People may have to travel. Hotels may have to checked into, or even found at short notice. Food may have to be organised that evening and the clock is ticking for everyone on that team.

The inspection timetable is an important one. Discuss it with your OI/HMI in that initial call and suggest meetings with people you'd like them to see. Of course, agree to joint observations, but ask if it would be OK for your SLT to help inspectors to choose which classrooms to visit – more important in a secondary. You might just want to keep inspectors out of a particular classroom, or two, if you can. There can be all sorts of reasons why. If a member of staff is on capability, or there is a supply teacher, that's not going to help the inspection and puts undue pressure on such individuals. In these cases, inspectors usually keep away. However, what if you know that a particular teacher's assessment is not where you would like it to be at that moment in time, or behaviour management can be an issue with a particular group, or a teacher has trouble following the school's marking policy and you are presently in talks about it...?

The inspection meetings I'd usually ask for are below. These were from an inspection at a large secondary school with a sixth form, but it is similar to what I'd ask for in a primary school. Substitute; 'early years' for, '16-19 study programmes', in this case. A, B, C and D were team members. I'd distribute the meetings amongst the team, appropriate to the number of inspectors. In some meetings I'd have another inspector with me.

MEETINGS TO FIT
1. Achievement (Paul +1)
2. 3/4 Middle leaders CPD/appraisal/areas for improvement for school (D)
3. Govs (Paul +1)
4. Staff appraisal w/ HT (Paul +1)
5. SMSC (C)
6. Call to LA link, or an external who can talk about the school (Paul)
7. Curriculum (B)
8. Attendance/punctuality (A)
9. Safeguarding check (A)
10. B&S Beh logs/ Racist incidents/ bullying/exclusions (A)
11. PP, Yr 7 catch-up funding w/ HT (Paul+1)
    SENDco progress of SEND/case studies; check procedures and rigour (C)
12. 16-19 Study Programmes (D)
13. Pupil voice (all)

There is no expectation from Ofsted that team inspectors have to do any pre-inspection preparation. They only get paid for the days they are in school, but as a team inspector, I would always prepare and most do, unless they have been switched to the inspection at very short notice. As a team inspector, I'd be anxious if I didn't get a SEF and a set of joining instructions, together with a draft timetable of what I'll be doing and when, before I set off. You can never be completely sure about Internet access away from home in hotels and you probably have no printer. Thus, I'm grateful if both documents can arrive before, say, 3.30/4.00. You can really help to relieve all your inspectors' anxieties and so start the inspection with the team thinking well of your organisation, if you sort these things quickly on the afternoon following your phone call.

By now, I may be travelling, or I'll be travelling early in the morning. The more relaxed I am, because my inspection preparation has gone well, the better I'll be feeling about the inspection and thus, potentially, about your school. I'll spend the evening going over your SEF, data and any other information you may have sent me, again. We may be in touch by email and you will send me the documents I'm allowed to ask for. This may happen on several occasions. So open a line of communication, be prompt with replies and appear well organised, because your LI wants to be well prepared when they arrive, especially around school data. Keep your inspectors close, but your lead inspector closer. You'll reap the rewards tomorrow.

3.2 During the Inspection

Ofsted's factual information, as to what will happen during an inspection is contained in the handbook (Pages 19 to 30). Let me take you through the inspection day(s) from a lead inspector's point of view.

I'll be there at 8am, or just before and I'll ask my team to arrive a little later, so I can meet the headteacher first. It's important I set the tone, which will be friendly and very much seeking co-operation. Inspectors are tasked with making good relationships with schools and especially with the headteacher.

I'd like to quash a pervasive myth here. Inspectors don't make their mind up about grades before entering a school. It's never happened on any inspection I've led, or any of which I've been a part. Please don't think this. As an inspector, you have no idea of what you are going to find when you walk through the gates of a school. 'Data is a just a signpost' is a phrase used by Ofsted that is very true to this point. I haven't yet seen all your data and I have no idea what is happening behind that keypad entry door to the right, or left, of the signing in sheet!

If it is a no-notice inspection, for any reason, I'll be in the car park, or close by the school at 7.45am and you'll get a phone call then. Be sanguine, if this happens, welcome the inspectors into your school, listen to the reason why they are there and to what they ask for. You may have a very good idea why they are there and it is not out of the question that the school may have invited them in. I have been on no-notice inspections where that was the case. It's hard to generalise for this, as no-notice inspections usually have a specific intent. However, the inspectors are now on your territory. Put into place any general Ofsted preparation as soon as you get a chance.

With my team (if I have one), I'll meet with you and senior leaders, to run through plans for the day. I'm open to suggestions at this time, as to whom we need to speak and you can influence this. The last thing I want to do is to start saying 'no' to requests from the school, unless I consider them to be unreasonable, as that opens up routes to possible complaints that I don't wish to open.

We'll then meet the staff, often in the staffroom, or hall/lecture theatre in a 'lemon moment', as I feel exactly like a 'lemon', asking for any questions at the end of my spiel and hardly ever getting any! Hopefully, your lead inspector will try to put your staff at ease and will not show the tension they will be feeling. Good HMI/OIs are experienced at doing exactly this, but watch the body language. If your lead inspector seems nervous, put them at ease as much as you can, rather than increase their anxiety; they'll be grateful. Hopefully, your lead inspector will say that inspection should not put undue burdens on staff, the team want to see typicality. As I've already said, there is little teachers can now do to influence the inspection grades over the two days, more than to do their day job, follow school policy and be positive about the school.

I'll then get out and talk to parents with my team. Suggest a position where you know the most vociferously negative parents tend not to congregate, although sometimes parents make a beeline for me. I can remember walking up to speak to a group of parents and being assailed by the most negative comments imaginable about the school I had just started to inspect. I spent much of the next two days investigating whether what these parents had said was correct. Eventually it became clear that I'd walked into a vipers' nest! Nothing the parents had said to me about this school was true. One parent was actually a grandparent who had attended this school and had hated it ever since. One lady said she'd taken her boy out of the school to home educate him, the school was so bad, neglecting to tell me she had three other boys in different classes, who were all very happy and doing well! It is possible to exert some behind-the-scenes influence here, because I have been approached by some very positive parents too(!). Parents will be encouraged to fill in the questionnaire on 'Parent View' but any parent has the right to request a meeting with the lead inspector. Some do. Some write letters and many are very positive. Few contacts have been very negative on the inspections I have led, though I have had to follow up some *'serious issues with the school and record its response'* (Page 18, Paragraph 55). There is nothing wrong with encouraging parents to contact the inspection team, as inspectors *'have a statutory duty to have regard to the views of parents and other prescribed persons'.* (Page 18, Paragraph 52).

THE TWO MOST IMPORTANT MEETINGS – 'SAFEGUARDING' AND 'OUTCOMES FOR PUPILS'

Different leads will organise the inspection in different ways. For instance, I liked to start the inspection with learning walks, pairing my team with senior leaders until break of the first day. However, I (and most other lead inspectors/HMI) always organised two things to take place on that first morning, whether it is a short Section 8, or a full Section 5, inspection.

Firstly, I'll check safeguarding procedures. I've already highlighted the documentation I'll be using and the documentation that you should be familiar with, but really, you should know this inside out and you should be able to demonstrate that knowledge with confidence. If you're making mistakes with safeguarding, pupils are potentially at risk and no inspector will have much sympathy. I certainly didn't. I'll be looking for gaps in your SCR and I'll ask you why any gaps are there. I'll expect training and procedures to be excellent and I'll look to verify what you say with (using that that lovely phrase 'triangulate with') all stakeholders and especially pupils. I will be punctilious in every aspect here; don't expect me not to be, so please; be spot on with safeguarding.

I rather wish the auditing of safeguarding was done by different people from Ofsted. This is another area that could be hived off from inspection and it would save precious inspection time. As a lead, this was the one thing that scared me about inspecting. I'd inspect safeguarding to the very best of my ability and my knowledge of procedures is very good, as it must be. But what if I missed something and the school hit the newspapers a few weeks later, for a safeguarding error that I'd missed? Where would I stand? Fortunately it never happened, but around safeguarding; 'there but for the grace of God' go all HMI and lead inspectors!

Secondly, I'll ask for a meeting about 'outcomes for pupils'. Next to safeguarding, this is the most important meeting of your inspection and it dwarfs the importance of every other meeting. You'll be well prepared via your SEF and that same SEF will allow a corporate approach to data presentation, amongst your leadership team, should I, or my lead inspectors ask them. And we 'sneakily' will! Especially during learning walks. That's when SLT guards can be down and during friendly chats, information less supportive of your cause can slip out. In consequence, ensure your SLT are speaking the same language as you throughout the inspection, but someone is bound to make a mistake somewhere and it's not the end of your inspection world! If your story is a tight one, slips by anyone can easily be explained. Prepare staff about conversations with inspectors too, but just stick to teachers and their assistants staying positive about the school. No more work than that.

However, when RAISE/ASP is produced, there's nothing wrong with emailing it to all staff, with a note that this is for information only. Say you'll never ask for detailed knowledge from any member of teaching staff, or support staff and mean it. No one else would and especially not inspectors, so staff don't need to open RAISE/ASP, if they don't want to. Some staff, however, will enjoy having access to RAISE/ASP, will feel more included and some will pore over it to see how the school, and especially their particular area (say, EY, KS1, or a subject) has done. There are budding data nerds amongst NQTs and simply sharing RAISE/ASP, without expectations, can be a very good way of raising data awareness amongst staff.

I'll be looking for your personal organisation, as well as knowledge about your data in the 'outcomes for pupils' meeting. This meeting is as much about the 'effectiveness of leadership and management' as it is about 'outcomes for pupils'. If I'm seeing you scrabble around for information and being naïve about aspects of your data, I'm unlikely to offer help and I'll be thinking you are not fully in charge. However, if you've sown the seeds of the grades you want via your SEF, this is the meeting in which you can be confident enough to persuade me that you are the 'overall effectiveness' grade that you say you are, via your pupil outcomes.

My advice is to not do that 'outcomes for pupils' meeting alone. I won't, if I have any team members. You can feel isolated and so can I. I'll get a team member to scribe and they will also be there to give me a break from being the main questioner. They'll ask questions too and they may well be as knowledgeable about your data as me. I'd expect you to have one other (or maybe two, in a larger primary, or secondary), with you in that meeting, but there may be just myself and the headteacher in a small primary and that can be tough. In that situation, if your chair of governors is data proficient, or there is another governor who chairs the 'standards' committee, or such, why not invite them to give you some back-up, if one can be free? Your lead inspector can't object and if they did – complain. You are facing a data savvy, well-trained, lead inspector and those outliers, transients and the progress of your current pupils could be vital in persuading that lead inspector that your case is sound. Two heads can be better than one. Show you understand your data and that you can talk about it well. Hopefully, following this meeting and by lunchtime, your HMI/OI will be talking your language.

Data is never the be-all and end-all of inspection, however. My team and myself will have gained a good impression of your school during our initial walks and inspection activities. I'll have asked the team for early impressions – a very un-Ofsted-sounding; 'how does this school feel'. I'll continue to ask that question though the first (or only) day. If there is only me, it will be a question I'll regularly consider. If the team feeling is that they are in a good school, but, on paper, the data doesn't look positive, there's a problem with that 'fit' and it may be that we are wrong and 'feel' is nothing like enough, or that the school is either improving rapidly, or last year's data were not typical. The 'fit' problem can work the other way too. If the team are coming back with a few horror stories, but your data could be interpreted as 'Good' on paper, something's wrong and I/we need to dig deeper.

THE REST OF MY INSPECTION DAY(S)

Notice first that I've separated safeguarding and 'outcomes for pupils'. No other inspection activities come close to matching their importance in determining your grade and that includes the 'limiting' area of spiritual, moral, social and cultural education. Get SMSC wrong, (and a few schools do get this badly wrong around their 'Prevent' duty, or unbending religious views in very strict faith schools, which may compromise their work in promoting tolerance of other faiths and cultures in 'traditional British values' – the so-called 'Trojan Horse' schools are the classic example) and this can lead a school down the path of 'Special Measures', but it is very uncommon.

Much of the rest of my inspection day, or days will be taken up with lesson observations and the meetings from my meetings list. If I've heard a good data story from the school and it 'fits' with initial feelings about what me, and/or my team is saying, I'll be wanting more information to help me to write a positive inspection report, that will back our eventual grades. I'll thus be instructing the team to lean towards the positive from now on. However, if my fears about the data prove founded, I'll be looking for the team to ensure that their EFs contain reasons why the school may not be good, or indeed, may be G4.

I have, in the back of my mind throughout the inspection, the knowledge that my report, or Section 8 monitoring letter, has to be consistent with my evidence base. If I convert your short, Section 8 inspection and your school eventually receives a grade of 'Requires improvement' (Grade 3), or needs 'Special Measures' (Grade 4), my evidence base has to be watertight in providing evidence for those grades. I thus can't accept many overly positive evidence forms and I can't write such positive EFs myself, if the school is likely to end up Grade 3, or Grade 4. Ofsted are very clear on this in training and on inspection. In determining grades, Ofsted say it is a corporate effort, but it is the lead inspector that sets the tone and the LI is the ultimate grade arbiter. The reason for me saying this is that if my evidence base does not fit the grades we all eventually give; it will be me that has trouble with quality assurance. A range of overly positive EFs won't fit with the grade given, so I have to direct the team in their EF writing. A subsequent investigation of my evidence base, could find my evidence base and therefore my inspection, lacking and a complaint could be successful.

Therein lies the inherent subjectivity of the inspection process. Either myself, or myself and my team, proceed with a 'glass half full' approach for the rest of the inspection, or we proceed with a 'glass half-empty' approach. My decisions on 'outcomes for pupils' and whether they 'fit' with what we are seeing elsewhere, is the most important factor. If this is a short G2 inspection, I'll make a decision fairly soon in the day, as to whether the inspection will convert and as long as safeguarding is OK, the 'outcomes for pupils' meeting will have been the major determinant. That meeting can be swayed by your preparation, knowledge and... nerve.

Inspections can be a battle of wills between lead inspector and headteacher. This is more often true in secondary schools, where the headteacher can be backed by quite a large and specialist SLT. This battle of wills can develop if the lead inspector's approach is not open and investigative and was perhaps more true of inspections and inspectors, before the summer 2015 'cull' of independent inspectors, than it is today.

The quality of your preparation and your proficient presentation of data can leave you playing a stronger hand than you may think. Important inspection meetings can come down to preparation, confidence, humanity and force of will. Early and good relationships – right from the first phone call with your lead inspector, can be so useful to you when it comes to push and shove around pupil outcomes – hence the inclusion of 'humanity' in that list. I will be thinking the same thing and my friendly and open early demeanour is there to quickly build those relationships for the potential battles to come. Research shows it is much easier to give bad news to someone with whom you have previously built a good relationship, no matter how quickly that relationship has been built.

Play a canny hand in your 'outcomes for pupils' meeting. It could be a meeting that determines your school's future. The stakes really are that high, if you are a G2/G3 cusp school. I've highlighted the different futures between staying 'Good' at the end of your short, Section 8 inspection day and having to fight a rearguard action where the conversion team is being asked by their lead HMI/OI 'is this school no longer a 'Good' school'. If your preparation via a persuasive SEF and data argument is excellent and is backed by a compelling presentation in the 'outcomes for pupils' meeting, it is far more difficult for me to argue against. In order to disagree with you in the 'outcomes for pupils' meeting, I have to set out an opposite position to you and justify that position through potential discord. It is here where decisions are made. Challenge reasonably, but have underlying steel that your SEF position is right. Don't leave this meeting to friendly chance, whatever you do. Prepare very well. Yours and your school's future could be at stake.

If there is no obvious 'fit', I'll not yet be in a position to begin to guide the inspection towards an overall grade and I'll keep digging and gathering evidence. I'll always give the school every opportunity to provide more data, but if you get into a position where I am less positive than you are about your data, your original plan has failed and you have to re-group. The inspection team can now see the same lessons, have the same meetings and talk to the same pupils for the rest of the inspection, but it is quite possible now to talk about the same grade descriptors to support one developing, eventual grade, or another. Every bullet point in the grade descriptors is subjective. There are no benchmarks. My report has to be backed by the evidence contained in my evidence base and overall; my EFs must back the grades we/I will give.

If I'm leading a short Section 8 inspection, as you are currently a 'Good' school, the determinant for whether I leave you as a continuing 'Good' school or convert to a G1, or G3/4, is 'outcomes for pupils', unless there is an overriding weakness somewhere else. There won't be an overriding strength, somewhere else, which will make me convert to look at G1. I'd have to have confidence that your data may be strong enough for 'Outstanding', or conversion would be a waste of time, no matter how well you school is doing elsewhere. If your pupil outcomes aren't strong enough, you will almost certainly stay as 'Good' for another three years, no matter what your other grades may have been, had conversion occurred (there are no grades awarded on a short, Section 8 inspection) and that inspection will not convert.

For me, conversion to look at G1 would take as a given that 'outcomes for pupils' could support a G1. I'll decide this, with my team, on conversion. The Section 5 team will look more closely at other areas as well to see if they provide sufficient to support to 'outcomes for pupils' for G1. Hence your SEF, your preparedness and your performance in that one meeting can lead your HMI/OI to execute a conversion. If conversion occurs and 'Outstanding' is on your HMI/OIs mind from the short inspection, go for the jugular! Don't let up on your original arguments to every inspector. The possibility of being exempt from inspection is there, so don't be one of the schools whose inspection converted, but the school stayed the same grade. What an opportunity missed! Use every argument you can, already created in your SEF, to persuade the team that the initial decision to convert was for very good reason.

I may choose the pupils for pupil voice meetings, or I may let the school choose the pupils. The decision is mine as lead inspector and I'll be more inclined to choose to populate/load those meetings with particular groups of pupils, if I have concerns about the progress, or welfare of that group. For example, if I feel that higher ability pupils are not making the progress expected of them, I'll want to know why. Same with, say, slower progress of pupil premium pupils and especially, at the moment and as a result of an Ofsted focus, high ability pupil premium pupils. These meetings do have the potential to upset a well-arranged apple-cart, via safeguarding concerns. You can never control what pupils will say and neither should you – one of them might just tell the inspector that they've been primed! Pupils may also be the best salespeople that you can have for your school and may confirm inspectors' positive views. However, if you get to choose the pupils, I'm sure you can see a solution to that potential safeguarding banana skin!

I may not choose governors, nor determine the number of governors, academy trustees, or academy sponsors (collectively 'governors' for the purposes of this book) who attend my 'governors meeting'. However, I'm always grateful if you can keep this manageable. Only once and once only, did I invite 'any' governors to attend (as I should) but without clarification about manageability. 11 arrived, wonderful people that they are, and the 25-minute meeting bordered upon friendly chaos, with everyone wanting to have their say!

FINAL FEEDBACK

I will ensure that nothing in the final feedback meeting comes as a surprise, as I will have followed the expectations contained in the Ofsted handbook (Page 25, Paragraphs 87 and 88) and kept you, as headteacher, fully up to date. Hopefully, despite any bad news, we will part on amicable terms. It is possible to do this. In my inspection career, I'm pleased to say that I never had a complaint from a school. I have, though, been involved as a team member in complaints and the pressure on the lead inspector can be horrendous if the complaints are personal. Avoiding complaints is down to the way lead inspectors inspect and I'm gratified to see complaints reducing, following the contracting of inspectors directly to Ofsted.

3.3 After the Inspection

There's not much you can do and as such, this section is short, but your lead inspector has to then go through the rigmarole of report writing. I'll not ask you to pity them, but I found it an utter pain and I'm very glad I'll never have to do it again. The hoops you have to jump through and the contorted, specific 'Ofsted language' you have to use! Did you know that there is a 22-page guide to Ofsted's 'House style'[32] and that all report writing must follow this to the letter?

Ofsted's information as to what happens following your inspection is in the handbook (Pages 30 to 32). There's very little there and what there is, revolves around timescales and complaints. Usually, you'll get an electronic version of the report within 14 days and it is published usually five days later, within 19 working days. However this is not always the case and it may require further quality assurance. Basically, it's down to Ofsted when you get your report and when it is published.

If you have to complain – and I sincerely hope you don't feel that need – you've probably left it too late to have any effect on grades. Though venting your spleen, if you feel your inspection was not done fairly, can be cathartic. 'Better than magnesium sulphate', as one headteacher I supported through a complaint told me (the report went nowhere in terms of changing anything)!

COMPLAINTS

Inspectors are expected to uphold high standards and to inspect by the handbook. By and large, they do and the standard of inspectors and inspection is undoubtedly higher, since inspectors were contracted directly to Ofsted from summer 2015. This required a cull, especially of independent inspectors and Ofsted were ruthless, discarding over 1000 of them. Some discards were much needed, as, in my opinion, was the process overall, but Ofsted also lost some excellent inspectors. Some of those discard reasons were unfortunately very poor, like one where an independent inspector's last school, 7 years before, was 'Satisfactory', Grade 3. The inspector had led over a hundred inspections between 2008 and 2015, but was discarded for this reason, even before doing the exacting test days! Some of the best leaders I've ever known have been leaders of G3 and G4 schools, but in 2015, Ofsted deemed this a limiting factor for ability to inspect and said; 'no thank you', to all of them. Thankfully,

---

32. www.gov.uk/government/publications/guide-to-ofsteds-house-style

that has relaxed a little and the January 2017 OI requirements allow leaders in G3 and G4 schools to inspect, under some circumstances.

However, the overall result of the cull was that inspections resulted in far fewer complaints. In the 2015-16 inspection year, the TES reported, in January 2017, that complaints had fallen by 25%, from two years before,[33] (when the reduction in the numbers of inspections are factored in).

Ofsted's latest information (April 2017) about how to complain is here:

> www.gov.uk/government/uploads/system/uploads/attachment_data/file/606844/ Complaints_about_Ofsted.pdf

It is the lead inspector's responsibility to ensure that inspections are carried out in accordance with inspection principles and the code of conduct. Within that remit, inspection teams can use their own judgement, but despite the fact that every judgement they make is subjective, those judgements must still be based upon handbook information. Inspectors cannot step outside the handbook and introduce priorities of their own. Most importantly, the HMI, or OI, who is leading your inspection can't step outside the handbook. If you have a problem with a team inspector, talk to your lead. In most cases, it will be sorted by the LI. I've had to do that before and it never escalated to a complaint. However, if you have a problem with your lead inspector's judgement – and in many primary inspections and all Section 8 inspections (if fewer than 600 pupils in your school) it is likely that will be just one person – this is different. What do you do?

You could complain post-inspection. Ofsted have a clear complaints procedure that you can follow if you have any problems with your inspection. It is detailed in the handbook (P31, paragraph 121) and on the Ofsted website. The problem is that in 2014-15 there were some highly 'rogue' lead inspectors about and yet post-inspection complaints led to a grand total of only **16** changes of grades in >8000 inspections of 3-19 schools (Schools Week June 11, 2015[34] and HMCI annual report 2014-15[35]). Was inspection really so accurate that inspectors got grades wrong only 0.2% of the time? Shocking.

33. www.tes.com/news/school-news/breaking-news/sharp-fall-complaints-about-ofsted-inspections
34. schoolsweek.co.uk/more-schools-complain-about-ofsted/
35. www.gov.uk/government/uploads/system/uploads/attachment_data/file/483347/Ofsted_ annual_report_education_and_skills.pdf

In other words, if you wait until your inspection is over to complain, your inspection grades are almost certain to stick. Therefore, strike while the iron is hot. Call the HMI/OI into your office (take control) and put your complaint to them first of all. Most lead inspectors are very reasonable and will talk your problem through with you to achieve an amicable and acceptable agreement to both parties. However, if you feel your lead inspector is being persistently unreasonable and it is affecting their judgements about your school in any way, complain directly to Ofsted then and there, before lunchtime on the first day. Call the Ofsted helpline on **0300 123 1231**. You have every right and you are not breaking any rules.

Experience from supporting a school that, on two sets of independent advice, one being mine, did exactly this, tells me that it can work and HMI will listen. Whatever happened in the background, after the headteacher had talked to a sympathetic 'duty' HMI, led to the Tribal lead inspector speaking a very different data language at the start of the next day. The outcome was that the school achieved the grade it deserved to get.

The alternative is to wait for a complaints procedure that won't wait for you. The report will almost certainly be published on time, despite your complaint and your chances of redress will be exhausted before any grades are changed. Ofsted and your LI are often in touch with each other through your inspection. The process is usually one-way; your lead inspector will call Ofsted for help on points of difficulty and they are right to do so. An experienced 'duty' HMI will help the lead inspector. However, those same 'duty' HMI are also there to respond to others and one of those others will be you if you call the helpline during the inspection. You never know how useful the outcome could be for you and you have nothing to lose.

APPENDICES:
MY PRIMARY AND
SECONDARY SEF
WRITING TOOLS

Appendix 1

Primary School – Self-Evaluation (SEF) Tool

The length of your SEF doesn't matter as much as the telling of a persuasive story.

There is only one purpose of a self-evaluation: to put an idea of the grade you feel you deserve in your lead inspector's head.

Don't combine this with your school development plan (SDP). The audience and purpose is very different and the SDP will hand your HMI/OI his/her inspection trails on a plate.

Start your SEF with a clear indication of where you judge your school to be, set out in a separate sentence. e.g:

WE BELIEVE THAT X SCHOOL IS A GOOD SCHOOL.
The rest of your SEF then forms a document to back that statement. Really, writing a SEF is as easy as that. For me, it's about clarity of purpose and too many schools write a SEF without a clear purpose. In consequence they include where they are successful but they also expose every weakness under headings such as 'what we need to do to improve'. It can then effectively become a series of inspection trails for your HMI, or OI and can be evidence that you are not doing things well enough. The SEF should also be written in proud and confident language. It is a document of information, but also of persuasion! Wherever you can, use positives from your last inspection with which to illustrate this.

Start with your school's context, but make this your Ofsted context. Then include information about your school.

A. Context

The second most important section of your SE is 'Pupil Outcomes', as this will contain the first sight for your LI of your evidence for skills on entry to the school and the progress they make from this and other starting points. (Most important is to clearly establish children's skills on entry (see below). On inspection, progress does not begin from the Attainment on Entry (AoE) of pupils to KS2, unless you are a Junior school. It begins from pupils' starting points – where they joined the school. In an Infant school, the establishment of these starting points is absolutely crucial. In 'Pupil Outcomes', make these baselines effectively unchallengeable.

Set out your vision here. Do it succinctly and say how this is communicated to all staff. If you have a vision statement, include it as a clear statement. The descriptor for this is the first bullet under what *'inspectors will consider'* in 'the effectiveness of leadership and management' (L&M) section of the inspection handbook (Page 37, Paragraph 141), but it is important to say this early in your SEF, in the context of your school.

Use the context statement to bring up the main strengths early with a brief introduction to all the 5 judgement areas and your judgement grades. You might also wish to say that you have improved considerably from the last inspection, anticipating that section. Mention strengths in: 'Safeguarding', 'Governance', 'Curriculum' and 'SMSC', so they are in the mind of your reader before they get to these sections later. This is your first chance to give a very clear initial statement of skills on entry to Reception (YR) and into Nursery (YN) if you have one and make it clear that progress across your Nursery boosts your Reception baseline scores via the children that transfer). **Paint this picture as low as you can evidence.** I've emboldened this, as it is **the single most important thing you will do in the whole of your SEF.** This gives the basis for progress across the whole school. The details can come in 'Pupil Outcomes', later. Mention the effect of transience, especially if any outliers have seriously affected your progress and attainment in RAISE/ASP. Use proud language throughout. This is your school and let that show.

B. Information about this school

The 'Information about this school' section from your previous inspection report (updated using the context page in RAISE/ASP) will give you much of the other contextual information you need. However, flesh out the deprivation in your catchment with LA Data and IDACI data.

C. Progress in meeting the previous Ofsted inspection Key Issues
Have a separate section for this to alert the LI to the fact that you have addressed these and that progress has been made. Use sub-headings for each one.

MAIN SEF AREAS
The next 5 sections are the 5 Ofsted new framework areas (developed August 2015, updated August 2016), plus safeguarding, curriculum and spiritual, moral, social and cultural education (SMSC). Have the latest Ofsted Handbook (August 2016, at the time of writing) at your side and use it for guidance on what evidence to include in each section. Choose the grade descriptor that reflects your judgement and evidence all the sentences in that judgement grade throughout, unless there are areas where you feel progress, or attainment is better than in the grade descriptor. Don't flag up areas where you feel progress is not as good and don't use language that would lead an LI to an evidence trail that wouldn't be helpful to you.

You may wish to organise your self-evaluation to reflect the judgement order of the Aug 2016 Inspection Handbook, but although 'Effectiveness of Leadership and Management' has risen up the order of importance, 'Outcomes for Pupils' will remain your key judgement in the eyes of your lead inspector. Therefore, I would counsel putting 'Outcomes for Pupils' first. It's what your lead inspector will want to read first.

Area 1.

OUTCOMES FOR PUPILS
This is by far the most important section for your next inspection. It should reflect this with the level of data you include. It is easy to lose the expectations of the evaluation schedule within this, so do keep the handbook close and use it as a check to see that you have evidenced each bullet within the grade descriptors somewhere within your SEF. There is a bigger focus upon the outcomes for **current** pupils in this framework. It is clear in the descriptors, so don't dwell too much on past data and concentrate more on showing accelerated progress with current pupils in all years (not just in Y6/Y2).

Have a short, prose, opening context statement in which you state your strengths in KS1, KS2 and EYFS in attainment and progress. This is where you need to make your overall judgement of 'Pupil Outcomes', based upon progress across the whole school (from the start of reception). Repeat the language you used about skills on entry again here and use that to judge progress across the whole school. Try to make progress across Key Stages and across subjects and pupil groups as level as possible. If one group is making less than expected progress' that can open a huge can of very poisonous worms and it needs careful explanation! Explain any possible area of weakness carefully. There will be a story to tell. Data is key (Ofsted now call 'data'; 'performance information'). Pack this section full of data and show you have an excellent grasp of it. Tables are good, but **explain** each table you include, with a **commentary** immediately following the inclusion of each table.

Don't be afraid to use other data, over and above RAISE/ASP. Inspectors are tasked to look at 'performance information'. Pre-inspection, they will have had access to your last two years RAISE/ASP data and to your Inspection Dashboard, but nothing else. They will have seen nothing about your internal, in-year, progress or attainment data for other years apart from YR, Y2, Y6 and Y1 phonics screening check. They will not have seen, say FFT data, or progress data from any other commercial packages. Use whatever data you can to supplement, or even contradict, RAISE/ASP data. If your inspectors will not consider this, complain and call the Ofsted helpline on 0300 123 1231 **during** your inspection. Do this straight after your 'Pupil Outcomes' meeting. If you wait and complain afterwards, you risk being ignored. So few complaints result in positive outcomes, or re-inspections. Strike while the steel is still molten, not when the ingot is set.

Use pupil/parent and carer comments and questionnaire data to back your judgement.

Possible G2 lifelines. (These are explained fully in the main body of 'Taking Control'. I won't repeat that information in full here).

1. **Explain the progress of your current pupils fully.** The Aug 2015 handbook and all subsequent versions included an increased emphasis on the progress of current pupils. Reflect this by including data for progress to date in that year leading up to inspection. If data from the previous RAISE/ASP report (and Inspection Dashboard) was poor, but leadership and teaching were already improving but had not yet had enough time to take full effect by the time of the publication of the previous year's report, this could be your lifeline to G2. Data may not be just improving in the current Y6 and the current Y2, but improvements may be clear in other year groups, and progress may already have been accelerating in those year groups during the previous year.

Stress these unseen (to your inspectors through their data) improvements and clearly explain the links to improving quality of leadership and teaching improvements. Tables could be prepared that can easily be updated straight after the inspection phone call with your latest data drop. If you can persuade your inspection team that a corner has already been turned in pupil progress, you may have a vital way in to persuading your lead inspector that your school is improving, or that last year's Y6 and Y2 data is not the start of a declining trend. Thus Ofsted can leave you alone for at least another 3 years, as a school that continues to be 'Good'.

2. **Transience (stability)**. Be very clear on how **transience** in through a Key Stage may have affected your data and also how **transience out** (easily forgotten) has also possibly affected your data. Next to attainment on entry, high transience can be the key to explaining why progress and especially attainment may not be showing correctly in RAISE/ASP. It may just provide you with a lifeline.

3. **Outliers**. The effects of outliers, which can be seen in your RAISE/ASP scatterplots, can be a possible third G2 lifeline. I hope your HMI/OI understands the effect that outliers – which could lie beyond your control – could have on your progress and your attainment data. If they don't; you must! By outliers, I mean the lowest performing pupils in your Attainment and progress RAISE/ASP scatterplots.

In writing your 'pupil outcomes' section, follow this pattern of sub-headings and information.

A. **KS2 attainment on entry attainment, then progress**. Start with a short context summary statement then add more context/commentary throughout, explaining any apparent weaknesses fully, but also highlighting strengths.

B. **KSI attainment on entry, attainment, and then progress.** Again, start with a short context summary statement then add more context/commentary throughout, explaining any apparent weaknesses fully, but also highlighting strengths. RAISE/ASP contains no progress measures from early years to the end of KS1, in comparison to other schools, only the numbers of pupils who achieve expected progress, or above, or below expected progress, in your school. This can leave a primary school which takes from a very deprived and low ability catchment, with many 'reds' in it's 2016 data, following on from blues previously, looking rather exposed. However, you may have had a large number of children whose cognitive abilities are lower than other pupils. It is harder for them to make expected progress and they are not expected to have caught up until the end of Y6. Argue there is time for them to continue their catching up, if your KS2 outcomes are better than your KS1 outcomes and you are laying the foundations for that whole-school progress in the younger years. If some pupils' cognitive abilities are such that they are unlikely ever to rise above low, Page 55, Paragraph 187 of the 2016 handbook applies.

C. Phonics screening check. Explain your results over time, explaining apparent weaknesses, but highlighting strengths. Suggest how strong progress has been from starting points to the Y1 phonics check (there is no RAISE/ASP measure, of course). If your YR data shows significant weaknesses in communication, language and literacy (CLL) then phonics check outcomes that are still below average in Y1, may still point to very good progress from low starting points.

D. Early Years (EY). Include your EY data here (not in your 'Effectiveness of Early Years' section, because it ties early years into overall school progress better). Make your case for skills on entry carefully and confidently, using the last Ofsted report's comments on attainment on entry as a guide, but bear in mind that things may have changed from that inspection. Remember that entry data for this particular academic year may not reflect the entry data of the current cohort, or the cohort that has just left (which forms your RAISE/ASP data), so dig back for these data and include them. It will be FSP exit data, from 7 years ago, of course, but your entry data may be based on the percentages of pupils in each 'Development Matters' age band, as it may be now. This can make for good and believable comparisons. Include GLD data for the last few years and from your entry data, to your GLD exit data, you have your progress across EY.

Always be conservative with any recent on-entry baseline assessments, as the DfE/Ofsted may use your baselines, in 7 years time, as measures from which to judge progress across the school, though recent confusion and a DfE change of mind around baselines, have rendered recent data very questionable. That gives you a good lever to introduce your own assessment data and present this as more robust and cogent than any baseline data you may have collected for an outside provider.

Have a weight of evidence to justify your assessments, including any moderation data that supports you. Don't be tempted to be expansive with GLD exit data; you could leave KS1 in difficulties when showing progress. Think of a nice, rising, straight line for progress across the school and not a line with steps in it!

If you have a nursery, organise your data in the same way; entry assessments to exit data. Don't over-egg your data for children joining YR, but ensure it shows progress across nursery.

Explain KS2 first, as it has much higher weighting in the eyes of the inspection team – it is the end of statutory education in primary school. These all have to be consistent. E.g. attainment at KS1 can't be 'average' if attainment on entry to KS2 is below average. Progress across KS2 can't be 'good' if AoE into Y3 is average and attainment in Y6 is average.

Within KS1 and KS2, progress in English, Mathematics and all the various groups need to be covered; SEND, FSM, EAL/Ethnic minorities, boys/girls, low, medium and higher attaining pupils. Be especially clear about the **progress** of disadvantaged pupils, disadvantaged most able pupils and the progress of most able pupils (a current Ofsted focus). It is not now so much about whether you are narrowing the gap with non-disadvantaged pupils over time in your school, whether you are narrowing the gap with all other pupils nationally and, as it was in the Sept 2014 framework. The Ofsted phrase is now 'diminishing the difference'. Explain fully why this may not have happened in the past and use current data as well as you can to explain why this is changing. If progress of a particular group and especially if the progress of disadvantaged pupils appears to be slowing that can spell trouble (use your current year's data to show the trend is reversing). A picture of few differences in progress (especially) and attainment against each group's respective national figures, or even improvements over time, would be great.

Any difficulties/inconsistencies between groups should be explained. If there standout poor progress of one group, address the reasons with that group's data and don't forget the importance of data from **current** pupils. Don't miss the positives! The 'stand out' may be some groups who are doing particularly well!

Don't miss the 'learning well across the curriculum' and here's where you can evidence how you achieve that in both numeracy and especially literacy by employing other subjects to help.

Don't miss explaining clearly how you ensure the pupils learn how to read well and how you have embedded synthetic phonics. Give data here on the progress of interventions such as reading schemes as evidence that any pupils who may be at risk of falling behind are supported.

Use pupil/parent and carer comments, any outside survey information (e.g. Kirkland Rowell) and questionnaire data to back your judgement.

Area 2.

QUALITY OF TEACHING, LEARNING AND ASSESSMENT

Start by judging where you feel this is and use the whole section to back that judgement up with quantitative evidence. No statement without evidence to back them up should be your mantra. If you say that CPD has happened, justify what has happened by quantitative, monitored evidence that it has had an impact in the classroom. Use specific examples to illustrate and link to outcome data from the 'Pupil Outcomes' section above.

State clearly what your own monitoring shows about the quality of teaching. If you have judged lessons in the past, don't be afraid to include this evidence, even though Ofsted don't give grades to the quality of teaching seen in lesson observations any more. It is your evidence and can be used to back your judgements. Thus, tabulate your data on the numbers and percentages of outstanding/good/satisfactory teaching since your last inspection and how this is improving over time, if you have this. If there is/was inadequate/RI teaching show you are addressing/have addressed this, perhaps ruthlessly.

If you have changed how you assess the quality of teaching of members of class over time, say this here and describe the process and the evidence you use. Nothing wrong with explaining how you use this to determine progression along pay scales here, even though it is something that will be explained fully in the leadership & management section.

Ensure that you are providing quantitative evidence for every sentence in the evaluation schedule grade descriptors throughout this section, if possible and that you are not just describing what you think is/should be happening. Good examples of where leadership intervention has produced improvements in teaching quality in a Key Stage can really help to give colour. Say how you have effected improvements in assessment and marking.

Use pupil/parent and carer comments, any outside survey information (e.g. Kirkland Rowell) and questionnaire data to back your judgement.

Area 3.

PERSONAL DEVELOPMENT, BEHAVIOUR AND WELFARE
In the report, this will be given two separate written judgements, one for behaviour and one for personal development and welfare. However, the overall grade is the lowest common denominator of the two.

Begin by judging the overall grade and then judge the two grades individually as written statements – exactly as your lead inspector has to in the report. Use the whole section to back that judgement up with quantitative evidence. No statement without evidence to back them up should be your mantra again, but use good examples of how you have helped individuals to improve, who came to you with challenging behaviour. If you say that behaviour has improved over time, you must back that with evidence that shows that it has improved over time; behaviour logs, exclusion data, bullying logs, racist incident logs all may help. There is a lot in the criteria for judging this section and you can use pupil/parent and carer comments and questionnaire data to back your judgement and as evidence for many of the sentences in the appropriate descriptor.

Your attendance data over time goes here and this needs to show that it is either above the lowest 10% (the percentage from the previous year is in the handbook), or that it is improving over time. Use whatever you can to evidence this improvement in the current year group. Disaggregate pupils who have left, but who are still counting, pupils who are/were on your books for a time, but who never arrived, school closures for illness outbreaks, snow days. Pupils who had severe illness and needed a long time for recovery: whatever you can to show an improvement from the previous year's figures. Few lead inspectors will wish to hang a school on attendance, if the school is clearly doing well. As such, they will value your evidence here.

Use pupil/parent and carer comments (and Parent View), any outside survey information (e.g. Kirkland Rowell) and questionnaire data to back your judgement.

Area 4.

EFFECTIVENESS OF LEADERSHIP AND MANAGEMENT

Begin by judging where you feel this is and use the whole section to back that judgement up with quantitative evidence. No statement without evidence to back them up should be your mantra. Don't be afraid to talk highly of the headteacher here, even if you are writing the section yourself. Use comments from others to do this. Leadership starts with the HT/Principal, but needs to be evidenced at all levels. Let each sentence in the handbook grade descriptors guide you and you won't leave out things like governors, parents and carers, safeguarding, SMSC (only highlight – it will have its own section; see later) and curriculum (again, highlight and have a separate section later). There is no mention of partnerships in the descriptor but that needs to be included here. You could use sub-headings for all these sections. Don't forget to link L&M to improvements in achievement.

The reasons for separate sections are that the bullet point criteria within the grade descriptors (Pages 41 to 43) require particular areas to be written carefully in your SEF. Some are so important, that they require separate sub-headings, as they are limiting grades. Two limiting grades are defined in the inadequate criteria for 'overall effectiveness' (Page 36). These are safeguarding and the promotion on pupils' spiritual, moral, social and cultural education. However, the handbook goes much further. In the criteria for 'Inadequate' L&M (Page 43) if any of these things are inadequate, the effectiveness of leadership and management is likely to be inadequate and thus the overall effectiveness is likely to be Grade 4. These are above and beyond the other major assessment areas and none of these will be given an outright grade. These are:

- governance;
- curriculum;
- safeguarding;
- the promotion of equality of opportunity;
- the prevention of radicalisation and extremist views;
- the promotion of traditional British values.

4a. Governance

The August 2015 and 2016 frameworks put an increased emphasis on some areas and makes more explicit the emphasis on governance. The bullets to which you should write this section are on Page 39, Paragraph 148 and these are the bullets upon which your governors may be asked questions. It is worth commenting on some.

A. Performance Management (PM) of staff – any data presented to the team should be in an anonymised form. A summary of the numbers of staff who are on UPS and the dates they passed through the threshold (and whether your school's PM has allowed them to pass through) is useful to the team, as are some examples of how CPD has been specifically linked to PM and progress outcomes for pupils. Governors should speak about the HT appraisal process. Don't put that in the SEF, but advise them that they will be asked. Governors should also be aware of staff's PM.

B. Governor's monitoring of the fiscal state of the school. Again this could come during the Governor's interview, rather than being included here. Up to you.

C. The extent and usefulness of Local Authority/Federation monitoring and support. The LI will ask for a phone/personal interview with someone from the LA, or academy chain who has good knowledge of the school. Information could go in the SEF and any LA/academy person should be well primed before the inspection conversation.

D. The quality of governance gets its own paragraph and it is important to evidence the work of governors around the bullet points in Paragraph 148, Page 39 of the Handbook. Why not get governors to write this section? It will help them to understand what they need to know, for inspection, but it will also have knock on effects for governor involvement, both in the writing of the self-evaluation and in the wider school.

4b. The Curriculum

There are two mentions of 'curriculum' in the bullets for what inspectors should consider in judging the effectiveness of leadership and management and thus what you should write this SEF section around (Page 37):

- *'the design, implementation and evaluation of the curriculum, ensuring breadth and balance and its impact on pupils' outcomes and their personal, development, behaviour and welfare*
- *how well the school supports the formal curriculum with extra-curricular opportunities for pupils to extend their knowledge and understanding and to improve their skills in a range of artistic, creative and sporting activities'.*

Don't miss extra-curricular activities, but also note that your section about curriculum should also mention how the curriculum supports other areas of the school's work, including: spiritual, moral, social and cultural education, the promotion of fundamental British values, e-safety and the protection of pupils from radicalisation and extremism.

Also, comment on the range of subjects offered and any extras you offer above and beyond statutory National Curriculum, (if you are not an academy and whether you believe your curriculum to be sufficiently broad and balanced if you are). If you are a secondary school that has had to cut your curriculum offer, take time to explain that your curriculum is still broad and balanced.

4c. Safeguarding

Safeguarding is so big a part of inspection that it has its own 35-page set of guidance for inspectors.[36] They must know it and so must you as a school.

Ofsted expect also instruct their inspectors to be familiar with two other pieces of statutory guidance in relation to safeguarding and thus, so should you be familiar with them too.[37, 38]

To go through the intricacies of safeguarding is too big a scope for this SEF tool, but if you get safeguarding wrong on a daily basis and beyond simple administrative errors which can easily be corrected on inspection, you are not doing right by the pupils in your school and lead inspectors and inspection teams will not be kind. Nor

36. www.gov.uk/government/publications/inspecting-safeguarding-in-early-years-education-and-skills-from-september-2015
37. 'Keeping children safe in education: Statutory guidance for schools and colleges' www.gov.uk/government/publications/keeping-children-safe-in-education--2
38. 'Working together to safeguard children' www.gov.uk/government/publications/working-together-to-safeguard-children--2.

should they be. Write safeguarding as strong, unless it really isn't, but if it isn't, you'll be very likely to be looking at Grade 4 for L&M and for overall effectiveness.

Worth mentioning your website and whether it is compliant here. Your LI has to state whether it is and also has to state where it is not compliant. To do that, of course, you must ensure that it is! All information that you should put in your website can be found on the government website.[39]

And it is worth following the link to 'advice on publishing information about your school's governors'[40] (Paragraph 30), because buried in this is what you should publish on your website regarding governors' interests.

If your website is compliant, say so. In addition, to help your lead inspector, add a sentence like this (or copy, as long as it is true): 'There is no negative information, safeguarding or otherwise, of which we are aware, on the Internet, or in the local press, from the RSC, LA, DfE, or police, concerning our pupils'.

4d. The promotion of equality of opportunity, the prevention of radicalisation and extremist views and the promotion of traditional British values

Follow handbook bullets (Page 141) and grade descriptors (Pages 41 to 43) in L&M. There are overlaps between all three of these areas and overlaps too with curriculum and with SMSC. If you are clever, all three areas could be subsumed within SMSC and/or in curriculum in your writing. Be especially careful here if you are a faith school. The key word is 'promotion' and there is direct reference to the promotion of traditional British values around tolerance of different faiths and beliefs. A display in the corridor isn't enough and inspectors will delve deeper into curriculum and past records if they feel there is an issue.

Explain how you promote equality of opportunity for all and how you promote traditional British values through the curriculum/assemblies/tutor groups/specialist curriculum days and especially, perhaps, through your SMSC curriculum. Refer to your 'Prevent duty' training and remind staff of their responsibilities here, as you

---

39. www.gov.uk/guidance/what-maintained-schools-must-publish-online
40. www.gov.uk/government/uploads/system/uploads/attachment_data/file/558622/2012_Constitution_Regulations_Statutory_Guidance__-_Sept_16.pdf

would all areas of safeguarding. Inspectors will check with them, but again, these are day-to-day expectations. Also refer to your staff's training in child sexual exploitation (CSE) and female genital mutilation (FGM).

SPIRITUAL, MORAL, SOCIAL AND CULTURAL EDUCATION (SMSC)
There are no judgement criteria for SMSC and it is not judged separately, but SMSC is very important in the new framework and inadequate SMSC would lead to Grade 4. Thus it needs its own section. This is a limiting judgement for overall effectiveness and information for the inspection of SMSC sits within Overall effectiveness (Pages 35 and 36). It is the only area of inspection that does so. As such, it should sit separately in your SEF.

What is expected of you is clearly set out on these two handbook pages, (Pages 35 and 36), so use sub-headings and write this to the bullet points on those pages. There is a great deal of overlap with the promotion of equality of opportunity, the protection of pupils from radicalisation and extremism and the promotion of traditional British values, which all fall within the effectiveness of leadership and management in the handbook and there's nothing wrong with covering all those here. It would save duplication.

Keep the focus on quantitative evidence and pupil/parent and carer comments – use those on Parent View too, any outside survey information (e.g. Kirkland Rowell and questionnaire data can help here. In addition, link social and moral education to behaviour and safety outcomes wherever you can.

Area 5.

EFFECTIVENESS OF EARLY YEARS (EY) PROVISION
Treat this as a section with an overall judgement which is arrived at after looking at 4 different areas. Give one grade overall; there is no need to give grades for each area, but you may wish to follow the requirements of report writing by giving a written grade for each area. Your lead inspector will be expected to do that when the report is written.

Organise your EY section into these four areas, as highlighted for inspection (Page 58, Paragraph 192):

- outcomes for children;
- the effectiveness of leadership and management;

- the quality of teaching, learning and assessment;
- how well the provision contributes to children's personal development, behaviour and welfare.

I have deliberately reorganised the order of these to place 'outcomes for children' at the top, to reflect its importance in judging the effectiveness of Early Years provision. The bullets in the handbook, (Page 59, Paragraph 193) are your keys to writing your EY section. Ensure all are covered within the four sub-headings.

A. Outcomes for children will again be the main driver for your grade, but this only needs a reminder here, as the main data will be in your 'Outcomes for Pupils' section. Mention the main points and stress, yet again, the starting points of the children and their progress across both Nursery (if you have one) and Reception.

B. The effectiveness of leadership and management. This will be very much judged on the strength of your progress data, but a new appointment may have changed things for the good very recently. Write L&M positively, if this is the case. It will suggest to your lead inspector that things are on the up. The statements within the first bullet (Page 58, Paragraph 193) are the outcomes of the effectiveness of leadership and management in EY.

C. The quality of teaching, learning and assessment is quite a wide descriptor. As well as L&M saying how it is monitored, you need to show how the Q of TLA:

- nurtures engages and motivates;
- ensures good progress in phonics;
- encourages enjoyment, participation, choices and decisions;
- encourages creativity and critical thinking;
- encourages co-operation, respect and understanding beyond their immediate experience;
- promotes achievement, especially in literacy and numeracy.

Examples can be a great help here of your curriculum provision helps teachers to provide experiences that can develop all these areas.

D. How well your provision contributes to children's personal development, behaviour and welfare is threaded through the criteria in the grade descriptors (Page 59). Use any questionnaire data, or comments from parents to evidence how good this is and especially how safe parents feel you keep their children.

Finally, the third bullet in Paragraph 193 asks inspectors to consider:

- the effectiveness of safeguarding procedures

Don't forget to say how you keep your children safe and how you know they are safe.

OVERALL EFFECTIVENESS: THE QUALITY AND STANDARDS OF EDUCATION
Oddly, an easy section to miss when writing your SEF. All your previous information should lead up to making this judgement, so use the evaluation schedule carefully in making your final judgement. Ensure your grades 'add up'. If the quality of teaching, learning and assessment are not 'Good' overall, your school cannot be 'Good' overall. If the quality of teaching, learning and assessment are not 'Outstanding', you cannot be 'Outstanding' overall. The grade descriptors (Page 36) are very clear. If one of your other judgements doesn't match your judgement for overall effectiveness, be very clear on why it doesn't, because of the information in the second bullets in each of the grade sections G1-G3.

Finally, good luck. Follow this advice and you'll have created a persuasive SEF, to show your school in its best light to your inspection team.

Appendix 2

Secondary School – Self-Evaluation (SEF) Tool

The length of your SEF doesn't matter as much as the telling of a persuasive story.

There is only one purpose of a self-evaluation: to put an idea of the grade you feel you deserve in your lead inspector's head.

Don't combine this with your school development plan (SDP). The audience and purpose is very different and the SDP will hand your HMI/OI his/her inspection trails on a plate.

Start your SEF with a clear indication of where you judge your school to be, set out in a separate sentence. e.g.:

WE BELIEVE THAT X SCHOOL IS A GOOD SCHOOL.
The rest of your SEF then forms a document to back that statement. Really, writing a SEF is as easy as that. For me, it's about clarity of purpose and too many schools write a SEF without a clear purpose. In consequence they include where they are successful, but they also expose every weakness under headings such as 'what we need to do to improve'. It can then effectively become a series of inspection trails for your HMI (Her Majesty's Inspector), or OI (Ofsted Inspector) and can be evidence that you are not doing things well enough. The SEF should also be written in proud and confident language. It is a document of information, but also of persuasion! Wherever you can, use positives from your last inspection with which to illustrate this.

Start with your school's context, but make this your Ofsted context. Then include information about your school.

A. Context

The second most important section of your SEF to 'Outcomes for Pupils', as this will contain your evidence for attainment on entry to the school, where you may wish to disagree with RAISE/ASP. That's a tricky path to tread, but it is possible, as we'll see. Inspectors will challenge you, if you question RAISE/ASP data, but be well armed to defend your standpoint.

Set out your vision here. Do it succinctly and say how this is communicated to all staff. If you have a vision statement, include it as a clear statement. The descriptor for this is the first bullet under what 'inspectors will consider' in 'the effectiveness of leadership and management' (L&M) section of the inspection handbook (Page 37, Paragraph 141), but it is important to say this early in your SEF, in the context of your school.

Use the context statement to bring up the main strengths early, so they are in the mind of the reader before they get to the 4 (5 if you have a sixth form) main inspection areas. Also mention strengths in: 'Safeguarding', 'Governance', 'Curriculum' and 'SMSC', so they are also in the mind of your reader before they get to these sections later. Point the reader in the direction of improvements that you are making, especially since the last inspection and that you have improved considerably since then. Make sure you give a very clear picture of attainment on entry (AoE) from primary schools here. If you re-baseline in any areas, introduce this and expand on this in the achievement section, explaining why you feel the need to do so. **Paint this picture as low as you can.** I've emboldened this, as it is one of the more the most important things you will do in the whole of your SEF. I know RAISE/ASP can be difficult to get around, but re-baselining can help. This gives the basis for progress across the whole school. Mention the effect of transience, mentioning if any outliers have seriously affected your progress and attainment in RAISE/ASP. Use proud language throughout. This is your school and let that show.

B. Information about this school

The 'Information about this school' section from your previous inspection report (updated using the context page in RAISE/ASP) will give you much of the other contextual information you need. However, flesh out the deprivation in your catchment with LA Data and IDACI data.

C. Progress in meeting the previous Ofsted inspection Key Issues.

Have a separate section for this to alert the LI to the fact that you have addressed these and that progress has been made. Use sub-headings for each one.

Main SEF areas

The next 5 sections are the 5 Ofsted new framework areas (developed August 2015, updated August 2016) framework, plus safeguarding, curriculum and spiritual, moral, social and cultural education (SMSC). Have the Aug 2015 evaluation schedule at the side of you and make sure you evidence each sentence from the judgement criteria. Choose the grade descriptor that reflects your judgement and evidence all the sentences in that the judgement grade throughout, unless there are areas where you feel progress, or attainment is better than in the grade descriptor. Don't flag up areas where you feel progress is not as good and don't use language that would lead a lead inspector to an evidence trail that wouldn't be helpful to you.

You may wish to organise your self-evaluation to reflect the judgement order of the Aug 2015 Inspection Handbook, but although the 'Effectiveness of Leadership and Management' has risen up the order of importance, 'Outcomes for Pupils' will remain your key judgement in the eyes of your lead inspector. Therefore, I would counsel putting 'Outcomes for Pupils' first. It's what your lead inspector will want to read first.

Area 1.

OUTCOMES FOR PUPILS

This is by far the most important section for your next inspection. It should reflect this with the level of data you include. It is easy to lose the expectations of the evaluation schedule within this, so do keep the handbook close and use it as a check to see that you have evidenced each bullet within the grade descriptors somewhere within your SEF. There is a bigger focus upon the outcomes for **current** pupils in this framework. It is clear in the descriptors, so don't dwell too much on past data and concentrate more on showing accelerated progress with current pupils in all years (not just in Y6/Y2).

Have a short, prose, opening context statement in which you state your strengths in KS3, KS4 and 6th form (even though you have a separate section for this) in attainment and progress. This is where you need to make your overall judgement of 'Pupil Outcomes', based upon progress across the whole school (from the start of Y7). Repeat the language you used in the context about attainment on entry again here and use that to judge progress across the whole school. Try to make progress across Key Stages and across subjects and pupil groups as level as possible. If one group is making less than expected progress' that can open a huge can of very poisonous worms and it needs careful explanation! Explain any possible area of weakness carefully. There will be a story to tell. Data is key (Ofsted now call data; 'performance information'). Pack this section full of data and show you have an excellent grasp of those data. Tables are good, but **explain** each table you include, with a **commentary** immediately following the inclusion of each table.

Don't be afraid to use other data, over and above RAISE/ASP. Inspectors are tasked to look at 'performance information'. Pre-inspection, they will have had access to your last two years RAISE/ASP data and to your Inspection Dashboard, but nothing else to GCSE. They will have had access to your Level 3 VA data, if you have a sixth form. However, they will have seen nothing about your internal, in-year, progress or attainment data for other years apart from Y11. Neither will they have seen, say FFT data, or ALPS data in the sixth form. Use whatever data you can to supplement, or even contradict, RAISE/ASP data. If your inspectors will not consider this, complain and call the Ofsted helpline on 0300 123 1231 **during** your inspection. Do this straight after your 'Pupil Outcomes' meeting. If you wait and complain afterwards, you risk being ignored. So few complaints result in positive outcomes, or re-inspections. Strike while the steel is still molten; not when the ingot is set.

Use pupil/parent and carer comments and questionnaire data to back your judgement.

Possible G2 lifelines. (These are explained fully in the main body of 'Taking Control'. I won't repeat that information in full here).

1. **Explain the progress of current pupils fully.** The Aug 2015 handbook and all subsequent versions included an increased emphasis on the progress of **current** pupils. Reflect this by including data for progress to date in that year leading up to inspection. If data in the previous RAISE/ASP report (and Inspection Dashboard) was poor, but leadership and teaching were already improving but had not yet had enough time to take full effect by the time of the publication of the previous year's report, this could be your lifeline to G2. Not just improving in the current Y11, but improvements may be clear in other year groups, 7-11 and progress may already have been accelerating during the previous year, but none of this will have been seen in RAISE/ASP, of course.

Stress these unseen (to your inspectors through their data) improvements and clearly explain the links to improving quality of leadership and teaching improvements. Tables could be prepared that can easily be updated straight after the inspection phone call with your latest data drop. If you can persuade your inspection team that a corner has already been turned in pupil progress, you may have a vital way in to persuading your lead inspector that your school is improving, or that last year's year 11 data is not the start of a declining trend. Thus Ofsted can leave you alone for at least another 3 years, as a school that continues to be 'Good',

2. **Transience (stability)**. Be very clear on how **transience** in through a Key Stage may have affected your data and also how **transience out** (easily forgotten) has also possibly affected your data. Next to attainment on entry, high transience can be the key to explaining why progress and especially attainment may not be showing correctly in RAISE/ASP. It may just provide you with a lifeline.

3. **Outliers**. The effects of outliers, which can be seen in your RAISE/ASP scatterplots can be a possible third G2 lifeline. I hope your HMI/OI understands the effect that outliers – which could lie beyond your control – could have on your progress and your attainment data. If they don't; you must! By outliers, I mean the lowest performing pupils in your Attainment and progress RAISE/ASP scatterplots on P21-32 of 2016 RAISE/ASP.

In writing your 'pupil outcomes' section, follow this pattern of sub-headings and information.

1. **KS4 a. attainment; then b. progress**. Start with a short context summary statement then add more context/commentary throughout, explaining any apparent weaknesses fully, but also highlighting strengths. Use RAISE/ASP data to the full. This section should be longer than the KS3 section and your 6th Form section.

2. **KS3 a. AoE; b. attainment and progress by whatever assessment method you use.** Then add a context or commentary statement explaining this. 'No table without commentary' should be your guiding phrase!

Explain KS4 first, as it has much higher weighting in the eyes of the inspection team – it is the end of statutory education (at present!). Make sure KS3 and KS4 are consistent. E.g. attainment at KS4 can't be 'average' if attainment on entry to KS3 is below average and progress across KS3 and KS4 is average. Progress across KS3 and KS4 can't be 'good' if AoE is average and GCSE attainment is broadly average. The trends and the wording of their progress and attainment descriptions have to fit!

Within KS4 and KS3, progress in English, mathematics and all the various groups need to be covered. SEND, FSM, EAL/Ethnic minorities, boys/girls, low, medium and higher attaining pupils. Be especially clear about the progress of disadvantaged pupils (Aug 2015). It is not now so much about whether you are narrowing the gap with non-disadvantaged pupils over time against all pupils nationally and in your school, as it was in the Sept 2014 framework (See 'Outcomes for Pupils' criteria Page 57/58). The Ofsted phrase is now 'diminishing the difference'. Explain fully why this may not have happened in the past and use current data as well as you can to explain why this is changing. If progress is slowing, that can spell trouble. A picture of few differences in progress (especially) and attainment against each group's respective national figures, or improvements over time, would be great.

Any difficulties/inconsistencies between groups should be explained. If there is a standout poor progress of one group, address the reasons with that group's data and don't forget the importance of data from current pupils. Don't miss the positives! The 'stand out' may be some groups who are doing particularly well.

Don't miss the 'learning well across the curriculum' and here's where you can evidence how you achieve that in both numeracy and especially literacy by employing other subjects to help.

Don't miss explaining clearly how you ensure the pupils learn how to read well and how they may still be using synthetic phonics in Key Stage 3. Give data here on the progress of interventions such as reading schemes as evidence that any pupils who may be at risk of falling behind are supported.

Use pupil/parent and carer comments, any outside survey information (e.g. Kirkland Rowell) and questionnaire data to back your judgement.

Area 2.

QUALITY OF TEACHING, LEARNING AND ASSESSMENT

Start by judging where you feel this is and use the whole section to back that judgement up with quantitative evidence. 'No statement without evidence to back them up' should be your mantra. If you say that CPD has happened, or that staff changes have occurred, justify what has happened by quantitative, monitored evidence that has had an impact in the classroom.

State clearly what your own monitoring shows about the quality of teaching. If you have judged lessons in the past, don't be afraid to include this evidence, even though Ofsted don't give grades to the quality of teaching seen in lesson observations any more. It is your evidence and can be used to back your judgements. Thus, tabulate your data on the numbers and percentages of outstanding/good/satisfactory teaching since your last inspection and how this is improving over time, if you have this. If there is/was inadequate/RI teaching show you are addressing/have addressed this, perhaps ruthlessly.

If you have changed how you assess the quality of teaching of members of class over time, say this here and describe the process and the evidence you use. Nothing wrong with explaining how you use this to determine progression along pay scales here, even though it is something that will be explained fully in the leadership & management section.

Ensure that you are providing quantitative evidence for every sentence in the evaluation schedule grade descriptors throughout this section, if possible and that you are not just describing what you think is/should be happening. Good examples of where leadership intervention has produced improvements in teaching quality in a Key Stage can really help to give colour. Say how you have effected improvements in assessment and marking.

Use pupil/parent and carer comments, any outside survey information (e.g. Kirkland Rowell) and questionnaire data to back your judgement.

Area 3.

PERSONAL DEVELOPMENT, BEHAVIOUR AND WELFARE

In the report, this will be given two separate written judgements, one for behaviour and one for safety. However, the overall grade is the lowest common denominator of the two.

Begin by judging the overall grade and then judge the two grades individually as written statements – exactly as your lead inspector has to in the report. Use the whole section to back that judgement up with quantitative evidence. No statement without evidence to back them up should be your mantra, but good examples of how you have helped individuals to improve, who came to you with challenging behaviour, can really help to give colour. If you say that behaviour has improved over time, you must back that with evidence that shows that it has improved over time; behaviour logs, exclusion data, bullying logs, racist incident logs all may help. There is a lot in the criteria for judging this section and you can use pupil/parent and carer comments and questionnaire data to back your judgement and as evidence for many of the sentences in the appropriate descriptor.

Your attendance data over time goes here and this needs to show that it is either above the lowest 10% (the percentage from the previous year is in the handbook), or that it is improving over time. Use whatever you can to evidence this improvement in the current year group. Disaggregate pupils who have left, but who are still counting, pupils who are/were on your books for a time, but who never arrived, school closures for illness outbreaks, snow days. Pupils who had particular health problems that meant they had to take a lot of time off due to their illness: whatever you can to show an improvement from the previous year's figures. Few lead inspectors will wish to hang a school on attendance, if the school is clearly doing well. As such, they will value your evidence here.

Use pupil/parent and carer comments (and Parent View), any outside survey information (e.g. Kirkland Rowell) and questionnaire data to back your judgement.

Area 4.

EFFECTIVENESS OF LEADERSHIP AND MANAGEMENT

Begin by judging where you feel this is and use the whole section to back that judgement up with quantitative evidence. 'No statement without evidence to back them up' should be your mantra again. Don't be afraid to talk highly of the headteacher/Principal here, even if you are writing the section yourself. Use comments from others to do this. Leadership starts with the HT/Principal, but needs to be evidenced at all levels. Let each sentence in the grade descriptors guide you and you won't leave out things like governors, P&C, safeguarding, SMSC (only highlight – it will have its own section; see later) and curriculum (again, highlight. The 'curriculum' section will come later). There is no mention of partnerships in the descriptor but that needs to be included here. You could use sub-headings for all these sections. Don't forget to link L&M to improvements in achievement.

The reasons for separate sections are that the bullet point criteria within the grade descriptors (Pages 41 to 43) require particular areas to be written carefully in your SEF. Some are so important, that they require separate sub-headings, as they are limiting grades. Two limiting grades defined in the inadequate criteria for 'overall effectiveness' (Page 36). These are safeguarding and the promotion on pupils' spiritual, moral, social and cultural education. However, the handbook goes much further. In the criteria for 'Inadequate' L&M (Page 43) if any of these things are inadequate, the effectiveness of leadership and management is likely to be inadequate and thus the overall effectiveness is likely to be Grade 4. These are above and beyond the other major assessment areas and none of these will be given an outright grade. These are:

- governance;
- curriculum;
- safeguarding;
- the promotion of equality of opportunity;
- the prevention of radicalisation and extremist views;
- the promotion of traditional British values.

4a. Governance

The August 2015 framework puts an emphasis on some new areas and makes more explicit the emphasis on governance. The bullets to which you should write this section are on Page 39, Paragraph 148 and these are the bullets upon which your governors may be asked questions. It is worth commenting on some.

A. Performance Management (PM) of staff – any data presented to the team should be in an anonymised form. A summary of the numbers of staff who are on UPS and the dates they passed through the threshold (and whether your school's PM has allowed them to pass through) is useful to the team, as are some examples of how CPD has been specifically linked to PM and progress outcomes for pupils. Governors should speak about the HT appraisal process. Don't put that in the SEF, but advise them that they will be asked. Governors should also be aware of staff's PM.

B. Governor's monitoring of the fiscal state of the school. Again this could come during the Governor's interview, rather than being included here. Up to you.

C. The extent and usefulness of Local Authority/Federation/MAT monitoring and support. The LI will ask for a phone/personal interview with someone from the LA, or academy chain who has good knowledge of the school. Information could go in the SEF and any LA/academy person should be well primed before the inspection conversation.

D. How the school has used the Year 7 'catch up' premium. Give any quantitative evidence you have to show that it has made a difference.

E. The quality of governance gets its own paragraph and it is important to evidence the work of governors around the bullet points in Page 39, Paragraph 148 of the Handbook. Why not get governors to write this section? It will help them to understand what they need to know, for inspection, but it will also have knock on effects for governor involvement, both in the writing of the self-evaluation and in the wider school.

4b. The Curriculum

There are two mentions of 'curriculum' in the bullets for what inspectors should consider in judging the effectiveness of leadership and management and thus what you should write this SEF section around (Page 37):

- *'the design, implementation and evaluation of the curriculum, ensuring breadth and balance and its impact on pupils' outcomes and their personal, development, behaviour and welfare*

- *how well the school supports the formal curriculum with extra-curricular opportunities for pupils to extend their knowledge and understanding and to improve their skills in a range of artistic, creative and sporting activities'.*

Don't miss extra-curricular activities, but also note that your section about curriculum should also mention how the curriculum supports other areas of the school's work, including: spiritual, moral, social and cultural education, the promotion of fundamental British values, e-safety and the protection of pupils from radicalisation and extremism.

Also, comment on the range of subjects offered and any extras you offer above and beyond statutory National Curriculum (if you are not an academy and whether you believe your curriculum to be sufficiently broad and balanced if you are). If you are a secondary school that has had to cut your curriculum offer, take time to explain that your curriculum is still broad and balanced.

4c. Safeguarding
Safeguarding is so big a part of inspection that it has its own 35-page set of guidance for inspectors.[41] They must know it and so must you as a school.

Ofsted expect also instruct their inspectors to be familiar with two other pieces of statutory guidance in relation to safeguarding and thus, so should you be familiar with them too.[42, 43]

To go through the intricacies of safeguarding is too big a scope for a section of this book, but if you get safeguarding wrong on a daily basis and beyond simple administrative errors which can easily be corrected on inspection, you are not doing right by the pupils in your school and lead inspectors and inspection teams will not be kind. Nor should they be. Write safeguarding as strong, unless it really isn't, but if it isn't, you'll be very likely to be looking at Grade 4 for L&M and for overall effectiveness.

---

41. www.gov.uk/government/publications/inspecting-safeguarding-in-early-years-education-and-skills-from-september-2015
42. 'Keeping children safe in education: Statutory guidance for schools and colleges' www.gov.uk/government/publications/keeping-children-safe-in-education--2
43. 'Working together to safeguard children' www.gov.uk/government/publications/working-together-to-safeguard-children--2

It is worth mentioning your website and whether it is compliant here. Your LI has to state whether it is and also has to state where it is not compliant. To do that, of course, you must ensure that it is! All information that you should put in your website can be found here:

www.gov.uk/guidance/what-maintained-schools-must-publish-online

And it is worth following the link to 'advice on publishing information about your school's governors', (paragraph 30)[44] because buried in this is what you should publish on your website regarding governors' interests.

If your website is compliant, say so. In addition, to help your LI, add a sentence like this (or copy, as long as it is true): 'there is no negative information, safeguarding or otherwise, of which we are aware, on the Internet, or in the local press, from the RSC, LA, DfE, or police, concerning our pupils'.

4d. The promotion of equality of opportunity, the prevention of radicalisation and extremist views and the promotion of traditional British values

Follow handbook bullets (Page 141) and grade descriptors (Pages 41 to 43) in L&M. There are overlaps between all three of these areas and overlaps too with curriculum and with SMSC. If you are clever, all three areas could be subsumed within SMSC and/or in curriculum in your writing. Be especially careful here if you are a faith school. The key word is 'promotion' and there is direct reference to the promotion of traditional British values around tolerance of different faiths and beliefs. A display in the corridor isn't enough and inspectors will delve deeper into curriculum and past records if they feel there is an issue.

Explain how you promote equality of opportunity for all and how you promote traditional British values through the curriculum/assemblies/tutor groups/specialist curriculum days and especially, perhaps, through your SMSC curriculum. Refer to your 'Prevent duty' training and remind staff of their responsibilities here, as you would all areas of safeguarding. Inspectors will check with them, but again, these are day-to-day expectations. Also refer to your staff's training in child sexual exploitation (CSE) and female genital mutilation (FGM).

---

44. www.gov.uk/government/uploads/system/uploads/attachment_data/file/558622/2012_Constitution_Regulations_Statutory_Guidance__-_Sept_16.pdf

SPIRITUAL, MORAL, SOCIAL AND CULTURAL EDUCATION (SMSC)
There are no judgement criteria for SMSC and it is not judged separately, but SMSC is very important in the new framework and inadequate SMSC would lead to Grade 4. Thus it needs its own section. This is a limiting judgement for overall effectiveness and information for the inspection of SMSC sits within Overall effectiveness (Pages 35 and 36). It is the only area of inspection that does so. As such, it should sit separately in your SEF.

What is expected of you is clearly set out on these two handbook pages, (Pages 35 and 36), so use sub-headings and write this to the bullet points on those pages. There is a great deal of overlap with the promotion of equality of opportunity, the protection of pupils from radicalisation and extremism and the promotion of traditional British values, which all fall within the effectiveness of leadership and management in the handbook and there's nothing wrong with covering all those here. It would save duplication.

Keep the focus on quantitative evidence and pupil/parent and carer comments – use those on Parent View too, any outside survey information (e.g. Kirkland Rowell and questionnaire data can help here. In addition, link social and moral education to behaviour and safely outcomes wherever you can.

Area 5.

EFFECTIVENESS OF THE 16-19 STUDY PROGRAMMES
Note your sixth form, as such, is not being inspected, instead, it is the outcomes, in terms of the 16-19 study programmes that are being inspected. However, there is nothing wrong with writing to reflect the four main areas of your main school SEF, as inspectors have to judge the effectiveness of the 16-19 study programmes, taking into account (Page 63, Paragraph 199):

- outcomes for learners;
- the effectiveness of leadership and management;
- the quality of teaching, learning and assessment;
- the personal development, behaviour and welfare of learners.

I have deliberately reorganised the order of these to place 'outcomes for learners' at the top, to reflect its importance in judging the effectiveness of the 16-19 study programmes. The other alternative is to follow each of the 10 bullets in Page 64, Paragraph 200. If you choose to write using 4 bullets above as sub-headings, ensure that you cover all that is in the Paragraph 200 bullets. Whichever way you choose to do this, make sure you give an overall judgement for the effectiveness of the 16-19 study programmes overall. There is no need to give grades for each section, but you may wish to follow the requirements of report writing by giving a written grade for each section. Your lead inspector will be expected to that when the report is written.

It is worth focussing on the 'outcomes for pupils' in terms of data. Remember: data is always king!

a. 'Outcomes for Pupils' in the 16-19 study programmes
Talk about on-entry data into the sixth form. Your GCSE data may not apply fully here, as the sixth form may take students from a much wider area, or be selective, to a degree. Paint this on-entry data as low as possible, taking into account your GCSE data and what your ALPS data says.

Talk about A2 and AS separately and be clear about progress and attainment in each. Use all the data you can to show the most positive picture to your inspection team. L3 value added data may not tell the whole story.

Celebrate your achievement if a greater proportion of students than average stay on to A2, especially if they are doing vocational subjects, or you've been successful in recruiting lower ability students, who may have left, if it hadn't been for your support. These students may, of course, affect your attainment outcomes and average point scores in A2, but in terms of inclusion, you are onto a winner.

If your NEETs (students Not in Education, Employment, or Training) are low at 16 and you have a greater than average proportion of disadvantaged pupils entering your sixth form, you are also onto a winner in terms of showing inclusion and celebrate this too (perhaps again!). It can be a very persuasive piece of evidence to the team of your inclusive outlook and how you have influenced students' life chances in a very positive way.

Finally, Paragraph 201 states:

> *'Inspectors will also consider whether or not arrangements for safeguarding learners are effective'.*

Don't forget to say how you keep your sixth for students safe and how you know they are safe.

Overall effectiveness: The Quality and Standards of Education

Oddly, an easy section to miss when writing your SEF. All your information before should lead up to making this judgement, so use the evaluation schedule carefully in making your final judgement. Ensure your grades 'add up'. If the quality of teaching, learning and assessment are not 'Good' overall, your school cannot be 'Good' overall. If the quality of teaching, learning and assessment are not 'Outstanding', you cannot be 'Outstanding' overall. The grade descriptors (Page 36) are very clear. If one of your other judgements doesn't match your judgement for overall effectiveness, be very clear on why it doesn't, because of the information in the second bullets in each of the grade sections G1-G3.

On Finally, good luck. Follow this advice and you'll have created a persuasive SEF, to show your school in its best light to your inspection team.